# THE PRIVATE WORLD
# OF THE LAST TSAR

# THE PRIVATE WORLD OF THE LAST TSAR

*In the Photographs and Notes of General Count Alexander Grabbe*

EDITED BY PAUL AND BEATRICE GRABBE

LITTLE, BROWN & CO. Boston and Toronto

LIBRARY OF CONGRESS CATALOGING IN PUBLICATION DATA

Grabbe, Alexander, Graf, b. 1864.
  The private world of the last Tsar, 1912–1917.

  Bibliography: p.
  1. Nicholas II. Emperor of Russia, 1868–1918 — Portraits, etc. 2. Alexandra,
Empress, consort of Nicholas II, Emperor of Russia, 1872–1918 — Portraits,
etc. 3. Soviet Union — Kings and rulers — Portraits. I. Grabbe, Paul,
1902–   . II. Grabbe, Beatrice. III. Title.
DK259.4.G73 1984     947.08'1'0924     84-19473
ISBN 0-316-32271-7

FIRST EDITION

*Published simultaneously in Canada*
*by Little, Brown & Company (Canada) Limited*
PRINTED IN THE UNITED STATES OF AMERICA

*For our children, Sandy and Nick*

# Contents

# Acknowledgments

We thank Her Majesty, Queen Elizabeth II, for her gracious permission to reproduce the sketch by Queen Victoria of her granddaughter, Princess Alix of Hesse, future Empress of Russia, when she was a child.

For their invaluable counsel, we wish to thank Dimitri Von Mohrenschildt, Professor Emeritus of Russian History and Literature, Dartmouth College, and founder and editor (until 1974) of *The Russian Review*, and George Tokmakoff, Professor of Russian History, California State University at Sacramento.

In attempting to key our text to Count Grabbe's photographs, we have briefly sketched in the historical background, inevitably leaving gaps in this complex story. We are grateful to the many historians of the period whose works we quote, whose insights have helped us.

We also want to thank our editors, Christina H. Coffin and Elisabeth Gleason Humez, for their kind assistance and forbearance.

Paul and Beatrice Grabbe
Wellfleet, Massachusetts
August 1984

General Count Alexander Grabbe, Commander of His Majesty's *Konvoy*, in parade uniform (1917)

# *The Photographer*

My father, General Count Alexander Grabbe, was born in 1864 in the Caucasus, where his father, the commander of a military force, had been sent to subdue warring mountain tribes. Such an unlikely place of birth amused the Count, but as it happened his whole career was influenced by the fact that the Viceroy of the Caucasus at the time was the patriarch of the Romanov family, Grand Duke Michael, the son of Tsar Nicholas I. Through this contact of his father, Count Grabbe later came to know the Grand Duke and his sons.

Like many other members of his family, Count Alexander Grabbe was graduated from the prestigious military academy, the Corps des Pages, quartered in the Vorontzov Palace in St. Petersburg. It was the custom at the Corps des Pages to select outstanding students in their final year to serve as pages to the Imperial family on state occasions. Count Alexander Grabbe was among those chosen. Not until after graduation, however, did he meet the future Tsar, Nicholas II. On a trip around the world in an imperial yacht as the guest of two sons of Grand Duke Michael, he met Nicholas, then the Tsarevich, in Ceylon. About that time he had also come to know and had been a dancing and skating partner of Princess Alix of Hesse-Darmstadt, the future Empress Alexandra Feodorovna.

Count Grabbe had wanted to study engineering, but his wealthy grandmother, the Countess Elizabeth Orlov-Denisov, insisted that he join her husband's Cossack regiment. As he had no means of his own, he had no choice. He married a lady-in-waiting to the Empress, the daughter of a cabinet minister of Tsar Alexander III. They had three sons. I was the youngest.

Early in his military career Count Grabbe became aide-de-camp to Grand Duke Michael. In 1911, following the death of the Grand Duke, he was promoted to *Fligel Adjutant*, or aide-de-camp, to the Tsar with the rank of colonel. During the following years he was asked to accompany the Imperial family to the Crimea and cruised with them in Finnish waters on the Tsar's yacht, the *Standart*. In 1914, promoted to major general, he was appointed commander of the *Konvoy* regiment — an elite unit created in the early nineteenth century to guard the Tsar. In this capacity he traveled with the Tsar to the Front during World War I, and stayed with him at army headquarters in Mogilev.

Father lasted as long as he did in an intrigue-ridden court because the Tsar appreciated his abilities as a raconteur and his tact. Significantly, he never proffered advice. My brother Nils, four years older than I, was aware of some of the difficulties our father encountered, and told me about them: a growing coolness in Father's relations with the Empress Alexandra, his disapproval of the government's use of Cossack troops to quell disorders and to repress minorities. Father's greatest difficulty was remaining neutral in a politically charged atmosphere. He served the Tsar until the abdication on March 15, 1917.

Count Grabbe was also one of Russia's early amateur photographers. Using an ordinary Kodak, he recorded the years he spent in the Tsar's service. Although he took many photographs during his lifetime, only about 250 survived the Russian Revolution. The pictures in this book owe their existence to a series of events in the early days of 1917. In March, the Petrograd home of Count V. B. Fredericks, former minister of the

Count Grabbe as a young officer loading his camera (1889)

Imperial court and trusted advisor to the Tsar, was sacked and burned by a rampaging mob. At the time, Count Grabbe was at army headquarters in Mogilev. When he learned what had happened, he offered the Frederickses our apartment at the capital, as the two families had close ties and he was planning to take Mother, Nils, and me to the Caucasus. The Fredericks family lived in our apartment until after the Bolsheviks seized power. In time they were able to establish Finnish citizenship and were allowed to leave Russia. Before they departed for Helsinki, the elderly Count looked around the apartment for something to bring Count Grabbe from the past. Knowing his friend's interest in photography, he selected a package of negatives and carried it across the frontier of the Soviet Union in an inner pocket.

The photographs in this collection have never been published before, except for a few that I included in my memoir, *Windows on the River Neva* (New York: Pomerica Press, 1977), and several that are official pictures. Identification of persons, places, and dates derives from Count Grabbe's notes accompanying the negatives. His own eyewitness comments were recorded in his diary and later in his journal. Captions and historical background have been added by the editors. Count Grabbe was able to include himself in many of the pictures by using a rubber tube that worked the camera shutter.

What can photographs of a period add to an understanding of its history? A confirmation of what is already known? A surer sense of the ambience of the times? Further dimensions of character and personality?

These pictures were exceptional seventy years ago. With time they have become unique. Taken with an ordinary Kodak, they show the photographer's pleasure in exercising a new skill. A modest man, my father would have claimed nothing more. Here, he is an unwitting recorder of the last years of the Romanov dynasty.

Paul Grabbe

# Russia in the Early Twentieth Century

# *Landlord and Peasant—*
# *The Land Nicholas Inherited*

Nicholas II ascended the throne in 1894. The formidable domain he fell heir to would have been difficult to rule whatever the government. Then as now its diverse nationalities were held together by force, and its bureaucracy was as stultified as it would appear to be in Russia today. Alexander III, a huge figure of a man, blunt of manner, had used repressive measures to hold the country together. When he died unexpectedly, the slight young Tsar, always in awe of his father, attempted to follow the same policies. But they no longer worked.

Though Russia had long been recognized as a world power, it was essentially a backward agrarian society, trailing Western nations in industrial development. It was fast catching up, thanks in large part to foreign loans. By 1900 it had the highest rate of industrial growth in Europe. New merchant and professional classes were emerging, as was a new proletariat; rapid industrialization was drawing younger men from the countryside to the cities. And while these industrial workers, wretchedly housed and poorly paid, became the shock troops of the revolution, it was war itself and the dislocations of war which would give impetus to the overthrow of the monarchy and, later, the Bolshevik seizure of power. The peasantry, with millions recruited into the army, would take the brunt of the war casualties.

In the middle of the nineteenth century more than half of the peasants in central Russia were serfs, property of landowners. In 1861 Tsar Alexander II abolished serfdom as an institution and allowed the newly freed peasants to buy land on the installment plan. The authority formerly held by the landowner was henceforth to be vested in the *mir*. This counsel of village householders had long regulated village life, even the periodic redistribution of land allotments. It was now to be made solely responsible for the collection of taxes, land payments and other functions.

The territorial subdivision higher than the mir was the *volost*. Some twelve to seventeen villages sent representatives to it. For years it had handled district problems beyond the scope of the individual mir. Utilizing these existing structures of rural self-government, Alexander II added a major innovation: the regional assembly, or *zemstvo*. To the zemstvo council, peasants would be elected from the volost level. Nobility, merchants, and townspeople also would be elected to the new assembly. Dimitri Von Mohrenschildt observes that Alexander II inaugurated the zemstvos "in recognition of the necessity to decentralize the administration of the empire."

The zemstvo did much to improve conditions in rural Russia, especially in the field of elementary education. By 1917 about 45 percent of the people were literate, compared with about 20 percent in 1861. According to George Vernadsky, the introduction of the zemstvo assembly "created . . . real local self-government without regard to class."

Alexander II's reforms, unfortunately, did not go far enough. While the peasant was allowed to buy land, title to the land was held in trust for him by the mir. Until 1906 he could not even leave the village without a passport from the mir.

In the years before World War I the peasant's condition improved. Sir Bernard Pares says that the years 1907 to 1914 were "the most prosperous period in Russian history," and adds that taxation was shifting from the rural population to the growing industry. Agricultural reforms also were helping. Yet the peasant's buying power was still low. Land allotments were not large enough, in light of population increases. Pressed for land, some peasants were coming to feel that if the government would not give land to them, they would simply take it at the first opportunity. After all, as many an older peasant believed, the land his ancestors had tilled for generations was really his anyway.

Peasant women readily allowed themselves to be photographed, but the men stayed away, fearing bad luck. Religious pilgrims — *stranniki* — such as the one in right foreground, staff and alms cup as their sole possessions, were treated by the peasants with earthy familiarity but also with a certain respect. They seemed "closer to God." These peasants are photographed outside the church at Vasilievskoye, the Grabbe family estate in Smolensk (1908).

Peasant and landlord, although neighbors, lived in totally different worlds. They occasionally came upon one another in the country-side, as Count Grabbe's camera records (1908).

Count Grabbe's sons Nils and Paul are rowed on an artificial lake fronting the manor house at Vasilievskoye, the Grabbe summer home.

Vasilievskoye had been built a century earlier by Count Grabbe's great-grandfather, General Count Vasili Vasilievich Orlov-Denisov, one of the heroes of the Napoleonic war. In *War and Peace*, Tolstoy credits Orlov-Denisov with helping to turn the tide of war in favor of the Russians by his predawn attack on Marshal Murat's forces at Tarutino near Moscow.

While Vasilievskoye was burned down by an arsonist in 1913, another Grabbe manor house was sacked by peasants after the Revolution. On that occasion, books were thrown out of second-story windows and the house was gutted with fire (1908).

On an estate such as Vasilievskoye, peasant women from nearby villages came as day workers to help with the haying (1909).

Countess Grabbe, mistress of the estate, attempts conversation
with a group of peasant women. Class differences, emphasized by
differences in dress, manners, and speech, made for mutual dis-
trust. The gulf sometimes seemed unbridgeable (1909).

Peasant men came to see Count Grabbe with a petition or griev-
ance. Their words were respectful, their tone surly. Count Grabbe
addressed them with exaggerated cheerfulness, later referred to
them as disagreeable characters (1908).

Nikita, the retired head coachman at Vasilievskoye, who taught the Grabbe children about horses and fishing and how to read the weather. Here, he is pointing to an old carriage usually kept in the carriage house, seen in background. The cap he wears was a present from Count Grabbe (1909).

Christianity was brought to Russia from Byzantium in A.D. 988, six centuries after Western Europe was Christianized. As in Byzantium, there came a close union between church and state. This old wooden church was near Smolensk (1908).

Rural clergy of the Russian Orthodox Church, a deacon, a priest, and a reader, stand in front of a group of peasants (1908).

By and large peasants believed that the Tsar was God's anointed representative, their "Little Father." Many saw in the clergy a direct link between them and their sovereign.

Church services and religious processions provided still other occasions for landlord and peasant to see each other. A procession bearing an icon, as pictured here at Vasilievskoye, might pass the manor house on a holy day. As the peasants came by, the Grabbe family at tea on the veranda watched in silence, uncomfortably aware that "there was nothing to say to them nor they to us." During all the years the Grabbe children lived in close proximity, they knew no peasant children.

The handwriting in left-hand corner of the picture is Count Grabbe's notation on the negative (1908).

Members of the village *mir* with the *starosta*, the town elder, center, near Vasilievskoye (1908).

Matriona, former household serf, who had worked as scullery maid
at Vasilievskoye, visits the estate with her granddaughter (1908).

On the left bank of the river Luká, a minor tributary of the Dnieper in the Smolensk area, lay Count Grabbe's 4,000-acre estate, Vasilievskoye, with its steward, staff of servants, horses, stables, carriages, greenhouses, tutors and governesses, tennis courts. . . .

On the opposite bank farther downstream stood the village of Gódnevo, population 200: wooden huts, just enough land to get by, some chickens, cows, and other barnyard animals, but no school, no dispensary, no fire-fighting equipment other than buckets dipped in the river (1909).

Peasant woman washing clothes in river near Vasilievskoye while pregnant daughter stands by (1909)

Peasant women who did the haying on the estate sometimes came to the pantry for drinking water or a chat with the servants, who offered them tea. Unlike their menfolk, they had no hesitancy in entering the manor house (1908).

Count Orlov-Denisov had built this church at Vasilievskoye in the early 1800s for his family and for peasants of neighboring villages. Most of the worshipers came from Gódnevo, half a mile down the hill. Though not one of the poorer villages in the area, Gódnevo did not have a church of its own (1909).

After the Tsar's abdication in 1917, peasants throughout Russia, including those shown here, lost no time in taking over the lands of private owners. They acted peacefully at first; land committees withheld labor from landowners and used other pressures. Within a few months, however, violence became pervasive and many landowners' homes were burned to the ground.

# The Imperial Court

In contrast to the poverty of the Russian peasantry and the city workers was the splendor of the traditional Imperial court at St. Petersburg. "Until I became aide-de-camp to the Emperor and had served a while," notes Count Grabbe, "I had only a vague notion of the nature and composition of the Imperial court. I certainly had no idea that there were so many high-ranking officials connected with it."

Some 1,500 dignitaries in all were officials of the court, many drawn from the military. Most held purely honorary office, had no specific duties, and rarely got a glimpse of the Tsar. They appeared once or twice a year on state occasions dressed in full regalia. In this group were 300 chamberlains, 300 gentlemen-in-waiting, and more than 100 persons attached to Their Majesties or other members of the Imperial family.

The court attire worn by these dignitaries was resplendent. The palatial setting of a ball at the Winter Palace, the flowers brought from the Crimea and the French Riviera, the bejeweled uniforms, each of a different hue, created a dazzling spectacle. Meriel Buchanan, daughter of the British ambassador, describes such an occasion — a ball she attended in 1913:

"According to custom [the ball] was opened by the Emperor and Empress in a solemn polonaise. . . . Heading a long procession of Grand Dukes and Nobles, the Emperor and his wife went slowly around the hall, keeping step to the wonderful measure of Chopin's music. . . . The Empress was a beautiful and stately figure in a sweeping dress of white and silver, a magnificent diamond tiara crowning her fair hair, and cascades of diamonds rippling over her shoulders."

Nicholas and Alexandra chose to live outside St. Petersburg at the Alexander Palace in Tsarskoe Selo, fourteen miles from the capital. Here they kept themselves in seclusion with their five children. Outside, sentinels paced and Cossacks stood on guard. Inside were few indications of the occupants' eminence: no pomp and glitter as on state occasions. The private life of the family was simple, routine, cloistered.

"Every weekend," says Count Grabbe, "a different military aide was assigned a tour of duty at the palace. I did not expect my turn to come very soon, but I was called almost at once following my appointment in

Alexander Palace, the Tsar's residence at Tsarskoe Selo

January 1911 and began my duties not without pleasurable emotions, for my new title carried with it special distinction.

"On the designated day, when I arrived at Tsarskoe Selo, a troika drawn by beautiful horses was waiting for me at the railroad station. It took me quickly to the residence of Their Majesties.

"Once at the palace, I took up my duties in the quarters set aside for aides-de-camp and then went to the reception hall where ministers and other personages were already waiting to be received by the Tsar. It was here that I found the *skorokhod* [dispatcher], who briefed me on the day's program. Without him it would be difficult to function, for he was the expert on court procedure and etiquette, knew everything, and alerted one in time about all kinds of forthcoming receptions and meetings and any events outside the palace requiring attendance by the Tsar.

"Following the morning reception," Count Grabbe continues, "I was notified that Their Majesties would like me to have dinner with them that evening in their private apartment. This invitation was the more unexpected since I knew that very few aides-de-camp were so honored. I could therefore hardly wait for the afternoon to end. But finally, as evening came, I was ushered into the dining room used by Their Majesties. Seconds later, the Tsar and his family entered and we sat down at the table — the Tsar, his children, and I. The Empress was not feeling well, had a special diet, and ate reclining nearby on a couch.

"The Tsar seemed to be in especially good humor. He was gracious and jovial, and I felt his charm at once. That day at Tsarskoe as well as throughout the next six years of close association, I found him invariably pleasant and gracious yet inscrutable. As I was soon to learn, even with persons of his immediate entourage, he seldom revealed what he thought or how he felt except in trivial matters, never showed like or dislike, and never made his position known on any subject. This reserve made communication difficult.

"That particular evening I was fascinated to observe the Imperial family in such informal circumstances, and I must say that what I witnessed impressed me deeply — I well remember the unconstrained atmosphere at the table, the naturalness of the conversation, the manifest devotion which the members of this family showed for each other."

Events in the country at large presented a startling contrast to the picture of happy domesticity here described by Count Grabbe.

Count Grabbe's sister, Maria Nikolaievna, Duchess of Leuchtenberg, maid of honor to the Empress of Russia, in Court uniform of crimson velvet embroidered in gold (1891).

As the Empress increasingly withdrew from court life, others stepped into the vacuum. Foremost among them was the acerbic Grand Duchess Maria Pavlovna (the elder, née Mecklenburg), wife of Nicholas's uncle Vladimir Alexandrovich. She held a glittering court of her own. To her elegant parties came intellectuals, statesmen, and prominent artists, as well as members of high society. Maria Pavlovna had a bitter tongue. Much of the gossip directed against the Empress originated at her soirées. Curiously, the current pretender to the throne, Prince Vladimir Kyrilovich Romanov, is her descendant (1904).

# Prelude to Revolution

In 1904 Tsarevich Alexis, the long-hoped-for heir, was born. It proved to be a year of reckoning for the Tsar. The war with Japan, provoked by the uncurbed expansionism of both sides in the Far East, was going badly. Political parties, long suppressed, were taking shape. Liberals sought a "free democratic system." Respected zemstvo leaders sent a resolution to the Tsar calling for a representative legislature. Nicholas brushed it aside and did nothing.

Early in 1905 many thousands of workers converged on the Winter Palace Square in St. Petersburg to present a petition to the Tsar for better working conditions. It included not only economic grievances but political ones as well. As they reached the square, troops assigned to maintain order fired into the crowd, killing hundreds. The incident came to be known as "Bloody Sunday." It was the first act of the Revolution of 1905.

Resentment swept the country, aggravated by losses in the war with Japan. Strikes spread. At the Black Sea port of Odessa fierce street fighting broke out. Sailors on the new battle cruiser, *Potemkin*, mutinied. Soon a nationwide railway strike isolated the cities, paralyzed the country.

To meet the mounting turmoil at home, the Tsar called back his former minister, Sergei Witte, who drafted a manifesto intended to placate the liberal parties and stave off the revolutionaries. The manifesto, signed reluctantly by Nicholas in October 1905, promised civil liberties, democratic franchise, a council of state and representative assembly — or *Duma* — to pass on government laws. Unfortunately, Witte appointed a notorious arch-conservative, P. N. Durnovo, as minister of the interior. Liberal leaders invited by Witte to join the cabinet, men such as Moscow University professor Paul Miliukov, refused to serve with Durnovo.

Strikes continued, culminating in the general strike of October 20–30; which tied up the country completely. To direct the strike, the workers in St. Petersburg organized the first "soviet" on October 26, 1905. Leon Trotsky emerged as one of its leaders. Once the harvest was in, peasants revolted, sacking and burning estates. With soldiers recently returned from defeat in Asia, the government repressed the revolt.

In the fall of that year a group of ultra-conservatives formed the Union

The Fortress of St. Peter and St. Paul in St. Petersburg seen across the Neva. Revolutionaries deemed dangerous were held here. The cathedral within the fortress was the burial place of the tsars.

of the Russian People. Opposed to the Manifesto, they maintained that Premier Witte had been guided by Jews. In their ire the Union instigated pogroms. During four days of violence in Odessa alone hundreds of Jews were killed and hundreds more wounded, property looted and destroyed. The Tsar wrote to his mother: "Because nine-tenths of the troublemakers are Jews, the people's whole anger turned against them."

After signing the October Manifesto, the Tsar honored his agreement. Russia's first national assembly, known as the First Duma, met in 1906 in the Tauride Palace in St. Petersburg. As the manifesto had promised, there was nationwide representation. Rancorous, this first Duma was dismissed by the Tsar in 72 days. He felt that the Duma tribune was being used to incite the masses. It also might be added that he was disappointed when many of the peasant representatives sided with the opposition.

On the day the First Duma was dissolved, Peter Stolypin was made premier. As an able provincial governor, he had won wide respect and brought to the capital first-hand knowledge of conditions in the country. He was keenly aware of the need for agrarian reform. A dynamic, far-sighted man, he saw the importance of cooperation between the government and the Duma.

The Second Duma convened in February, 1907. Even more hostile than the first, it was dismissed in three and a half months after Social Democratic members were implicated in a conspiracy against the Government.

Before convening the Third Duma the Tsar had the electoral law modified to decrease the number of workers and peasants.

With the franchise thus curtailed, the Third Duma lasted from the fall of 1907 into 1912 and managed to put through significant legislation. It gave peasants full civil rights and expanded the educational system. Stolypin, using his broad knowledge of rural affairs, introduced agrarian reforms aimed at making the peasants — in time — independent farmers. His program, hastened by a famine in 1906, gave millions of peasants title to land formerly held communally by the mir. He also persuaded the Tsar to open Crown lands for purchase by the peasants and to encourage peasant migration to homesteads in Siberia.

Of the Third Duma Sir Bernard Pares observes that "one could see political competence growing day by day. . . . The Emperor himself took a certain pride in it as his own creation." In 1912 Nicholas told Pares, "'The Duma started too fast, now it is slower, but better.'" The Fourth Duma, convened that year, would survive until the revolution of March 1917.

After the anti-Semitic excesses of 1905, a change was taking place in

Duma in session, interior of Tauride Palace, St. Petersburg. *Courtesy Hoover Institution Archives*

the treatment of the Jewish minority. Protests from abroad were having effect. In 1908 the Tsar's uncle by marriage, King Edward VII of Great Britain, a longtime friend of Nathaniel Mayer Lord Rothschild, chided Nicholas in a meeting at Reval. The British ambassador assured Lord Rothschild that there would be "amelioration." In 1911 the United States Congress, reacting to anti-Semitic policies, abrogated the old trade treaty with Russia.

During these years terrorism was on the increase and the Tsar ordered Stolypin to use stringent measures in the courts against Left terrorists. It was not long before terrorists responded with attacks on Stolypin himself. There was increasing opposition from other quarters of the empire as well. For reasons of national defense, he introduced a bill which gave a blow to Finnish self-government. The Finns were enraged when the powers of their Diet were curtailed. His bill to extend the zemstvos to the western provinces gave preference to the Russian peasantry there and antagonized the landowners, predominantly Polish, in the area. Though the Council of State, sympathetic to the landowners, turned down the bill, Stolypin maneuvered for its passage. Opposition mounted. In 1911 he was shot by a former double agent. It is still unknown who was behind the assassination.

That same year another baleful event occurred. Pursuant to his father's friendly relations with the French Republic, and in light of large French loans, Nicholas signed an agreement with France. "With more valor than discretion," observes Barbara Tuchman. It called for a simultaneous offensive against Germany in the event of war. The Russian army, the Tsar agreed, would be ready to cross the frontier fifteen days after mobilization. French strategy depended on diverting German troops to the east.

Since the strength of the German war machine was well known, the Tsar must be faulted for retaining the fawning, incompetent General Vladimir Sukhomlinov as minister of war. His preference for outdated bayonet attack over firepower accounted in no small part for the inadequate armaments output when war came in 1914.

It was in 1911 that Count Grabbe's service at the court began. During the succeeding years he had the opportunity to take the photographs shown on the following pages. They are introduced here with short sketches of the Tsar, the Empress, and their children.

# The Tsar and His Family

# *Nicholas* II

Nicholas II (1868–1918; reigned 1894–1917). There are devout Russian Orthodox Christians living today who revere the name of Nicholas II and say he was great in his faith, in his dutiful shouldering of a burden he never chose nor wanted, in his humble resignation to God's will, in his honoring of Russia's alliances. Their numbers, however, are few.

Many more deplore the deep conflict within Nicholas himself between his sacred trust as Tsar of Russia and the secular needs of his time. They criticize him for his weakness in allowing himself to be swayed by a naïve but strong-willed wife and a canny reprobate. While Nicholas always felt himself to be loyal to the Russian people and weighed his actions accordingly, on a personal level his loyalty was primarily to his wife and family — as many a devoted official discovered.

Could any head of state have brought Russia through the difficult transition into the modern world? Could he have given it a government worthy of world respect? Certainly the Russia Nicholas fell heir to would have challenged a sovereign of exceptional endowment: a rapidly changing society; a spiritually ineffective church; a peasantry ignorant, angry, and land-hungry, pressed by population increases; a nobility with no clearly defined social role; a foreign alliance against a more advanced neighboring state — Germany. From its economic geography to its oversized railroad gauge, Russia would have presented baffling problems to any erstwhile ruler.

Nicholas tried conscientiously to function as sovereign, yet his belief in his own divine right clouded his judgment. This belief, instilled by his father, was strongly reinforced by his tutor, Konstantin Pobedonostsev, Procurator of the Holy Synod. The Tsar turned to him for counsel during the first eleven years of his reign. According to General A. A. Mosolov, Chief of the Tsar's Civilian Chancellery, Nicholas "took his role as God's representative with the utmost seriousness."

In keeping with his belief, Nicholas never felt called upon to justify his conduct. When he seemed to be asking counsel, he actually was seeking opinions. His own intuitions, divinely inspired — or so he believed — were a surer guide than other people's logical arguments. Officials sometimes mistook his graciousness for acquiescence and came away thinking they had secured approval only to learn by letter the next day that they had been dismissed.

Similar considerations accounted for the Tsar's adamant opposition to a parliamentary regime. For how could he morally justify surrendering power — a sacred trust — to a cabinet?

Many have commented on Nicholas's composure and the dogged way in which he stuck to his position once his mind was made up. George Katkov finds a key to the Tsar's self-assurance under pressure in his "conviction that all his decisions had been taken with a clear conscience," dictated by standards of private morality Nicholas set himself. "His serenity," says Katkov, "was based on the conviction that his heart, which was 'in the hands of God,' was pure. In this sense the Emperor's character was saintly." His Christian ethics were characteristic of Russian Christian thought of the nineteenth century. And yet, Katkov hastens to add, belief in God's inspiration "proved disastrous in the conditions of the rapidly changing society whose course he was called upon to steer."

What was Nicholas like in private life? Count V. N. Kokovtsev, who served the Tsar loyally for ten years, first as minister of finance and later as premier, speaks of his remarkable clearness of head and swift understanding of any issue presented to him. Kokovtsev even remarks that with a different wife, Nicholas might have made a satisfactory constitutional monarch.

Many who observed the Tsar at close range comment on how hardworking he was. Sir Bernard Pares notes that Nicholas had a "great sense of order in the arrangement of his papers. . . . Though the Tsar lived apart from the people," he adds, "he was working for them all the time."

There is universal agreement on the Tsar's "conquering personal charm," which, Pares maintains, "had its basis in an innate delicacy of mind." His kindly manner seemed to convey to this British contemporary a kind of appeal "as if he were asking you to be pleased with his company."

In his notes, Count Grabbe also remarks on the Tsar's charisma. "Time and again," he says, "I was witness to the fact that even persons ill-disposed politically came away from an audience with him under the spell of his personality." Decades later, in 1984, the émigré historian, Dimitri Von Mohrenschildt recalled the experience of seeing the Tsar at close range in 1915. "His dreamy blue eyes," he said, "haunted me for years."

The Tsar's entourage was very small. He saw few people informally. Some relatives and two or three other individuals could dispense with the formality of requesting an audience through proper court channels. Cab-

The Tsar in the Caucasus during review of Kuban Cossacks, talks to commander of regiment (1914).

It meant a lot to Nicholas to be in touch with his soldiers, with whom he closely identified. He was proud of his colonel's epaulets, conferred by his father for army service in his youth. Here he talks to participants of the battle in late 1914 in which the Russians put the Ninth Turkish Army temporarily out of action. The Cossack commander is second from the right.

The Tsar hurries from the radio room of his yacht, the *Standart*, gripping a sheaf of dispatches. His serious and expeditious manner was characteristic when he was engaged in matters of state. The black armbands are worn in mourning for King Frederick VIII of Denmark. General Voyeikov, a military aide, is in the background (1912).

inet members and other officials came by appointment and confined their conversation to reports in hand.

Only a few senior officials had daily informal contact with the Tsar. Foremost among them was Count Vladimir Borisovich Fredericks, Minister of the Imperial Court. A nobleman of Swedish ancestry, he had commanded the elite regiment of the Horse Guards before he became minister in 1897. Long familiar with court life, he was the only official the Tsar trusted implicitly. Benign in his relations with Nicholas and his wife, he privately addressed them as *mes enfants*. Fredericks combined polished manners with an independent cast of mind. In the words of General Sir John Hanbury-Williams, head of the British military mission at Russian army headquarters during World War I, "he was a fine, gallant old gentleman."

Count Grabbe recalls that "when in 1915 the regiment of Horse Guards was ordered by the Tsar to take part in a review, tradition decreed that Count Fredericks, honorary head of one of the regiment's squadrons, lead it on horseback. Countess Fredericks, alarmed on hearing of this prospect, appealed to the Empress, begging her to ask the Tsar to dissuade her husband, now in his mid-seventies, from taking part in the review. The Tsar, also concerned, agreed, but the aged Count was adamant.

"'Nobody is going to tell me what is proper or not proper for me to do,' he declared. So he rode in the review, and when his squadron came abreast of the Tsar, he galloped smartly ahead and around to take his place at the sovereign's side, executing the maneuver in great style."

Count Fredericks headed a group of senior court officials who included among others the Grand Marshal of the Court, Count Paul Benckendorff; the Tsar's Flag Captain, Admiral Nilov; the commander of the *Konvoy* regiment, Count Alexander Grabbe; the Palace Commandant, General Vladimir Voyeikov, Count Fredericks' son-in-law; the Court Marshal, Prince V. Dolgoruky; the head of the Tsar's Private Secretariat, Colonel Narishkin; and Count Dimitri Sheremetiev.

Count Grabbe notes that even persons in these key positions felt to some extent tongue-tied in conversation with the Tsar. With members of his suite as with his ministers, Nicholas did not invite discussion on subjects unrelated to their functions. Accordingly, officials kept their conversation light and inconsequential when in his presence.

With men of his suite so constrained, the Tsar cut himself off from the last remaining channel of information about conditions in the country and the growing anger and frustration of the people. This isolation made him ever more receptive to advice from the Empress and the persons to whom she listened.

Nicholas believed that the simple people of Russia stood behind
him. During his walks, says Count Grabbe, he sought out occasions to meet with peasants to confirm his faith in their devotion.
Such an occasion is recorded here. Behind the Tsar are members of
his suite; Count Grabbe in left foreground (1916).

The Tsar in the environs of Mogilev — a moment for reflection in
the quiet of the countryside. A manually operated ferry crosses the
Dnieper (1916).

One of the Tsar's marked characteristics was his love of nature and the out-of-doors acquired in a childhood spent in the country at the Gatchina Palace. "Physical exercise," remarks Pares, "was an absolute necessity to him. . . . He found his greatest pleasure with his gun in the woods or swimming or rowing." Here he rows on the Dnieper river near Mogilev (1916).

A man of simple tastes, the Tsar liked the simple food at army headquarters such as cabbage soup and kasha (buckwheat groats) and other traditional Russian dishes so different from the creations of the French chef at Tsarskoe Selo.

Clockwise: Count Sheremetiev, Count Grabbe, Pierre Gilliard, tutor to the Tsarevich, unidentified aide, Tsarevich Alexis, the Tsar, and Prince Igor Konstantinovich, Romanov kin (1918)

Nicholas was an exemplary family man. Not only was he a loving
husband but a devoted father. His favorite company everywhere
was his children, "to whom," says Pares, "he was at once Emperor,
father, and comrade." In the picture above, father and daughters,
out for a sail on the Dnieper, would seem to be in a somber mood.
Left to right, Anastasia, Olga, and Maria (1916)

*Konvoy* trumpeters and a private in a field near Mogilev (1916)

The *Konvoy* was an elite Cossack regiment created to guard the Tsar. This service became necessary early in the nineteenth century when Alexander I, observing military action, was nearly captured by Napoleon's army. In more recent times, the task of protecting the Tsar became the responsibility of the secret service, and the *Konvoy* assumed a function that was primarily ceremonial.

*Konvoy* privates stand guard near folding stairs at the entrance to the Tsar's railroad car (1915). The black cloak each wears is a *bourka*, traditional Caucasian garb.

# *Alexandra Feodorovna*

Empress Alexandra Feodorovna (1872–1918). As a young officer, Tsar-evich Nicholas fell deeply in love with the beautiful German Princess Alix of Hesse-Darmstadt and chose her for his bride despite his parents' objections. Count Grabbe tells us that "Princess Alix had barely become Tsar-evich Nicholas's fiancée before she had to appear in mourning at the bier of Tsar Alexander III, father of her betrothed. And before she had had the opportunity to become acquainted with the traditions and habits of her new fatherland, she was crowned Empress Alexandra Feodorovna of Russia.

"By nature high-strung, timid, and secretive, she was judged by some in Russia to be cold and unfriendly, and was compared unfavorably with the Dowager Empress Maria Feodorovna."

In turn she rejected Russian high society, considering it decadent, and persuaded Nicholas to move his residence out of the capital to Tsarskoe Selo. There she wrapped Nicholas and her family around her like a cocoon and devoted herself to bolstering her husband's faith in autocratic rule.

On November 26, 1894, when her granddaughter married Nicholas, Queen Victoria wrote in her journal: "How I thought of darling Alicky and how impossible it seemed that that gentle little simple Alicky should be the Great Empress of Russia."

In the days of her youth Alix liked to visit Windsor Castle and came to prefer the English language and English ways. She was devoted to her English nanny, Jackson. In the provincial world of a small German duchy she was brought up as a Lutheran. Staunch in her faith, she found it difficult to change to the Russian Orthodox religion, a requirement for her marriage to the future Tsar. Cousin Willy, the German Kaiser, did his best to persuade her. After months of study with a Russian priest in England, she took the step, changing her name to Alexandra Feodorovna. She embraced her new religion fervently.

Following the birth of four daughters, Alexandra's anxiety to give the Tsar an heir led her to consult mystics of questionable character. One might infer that she did not know that as a granddaughter of Queen Victoria she might be a carrier of hemophilia. However that may be, after the joyful birth of the Tsarevich Alexis, it was discovered that he had

41

A sketch of Princess Alix of Hesse as a child by her grandmother, Queen Victoria. *Sketchbook of Queen Victoria in the Royal Collection, Windsor Castle*

*Copyright reserved. Reproduced by gracious permission of Her Majesty the Queen.*

inherited the baneful disease. When the child suffered an attack, it was found that a peasant healer known as Rasputin could allay the bleeding.

By the time Count Grabbe took these photographs, the strains of her son's illness had ravaged Alexandra Feodorovna's good looks, affected her heart, and made her a semirecluse. Apart from early official pictures of her as a resplendently crowned and bejeweled empress, photographs of her are scarce. The unsmiling, almost grim, snapshots here are among the few late pictures of her.

Few Russians knew Alexandra. Of those contemporaries who have written about her, the most levelheaded was her faithful lady-in-waiting Baroness Sophie Buxhoeveden. In her biography of the Empress, the baroness speaks plainly: "I knew her good qualities and her weaknesses. . . . Her want of political experience, her trust in the innate good of humanity made her commit many political errors." She notes that the Empress "acted largely on impulse" and adds that "when he [the Tsar] disagreed, he did not like to give a direct refusal to her but went his own way in silence."

Alexandra avoided state functions as much as possible. Some said that she neglected her duties as empress. Few of her friends were distinguished. The closest, Anna Vyrubova, daughter of a minor court functionary and composer, happened to live near the country estate of Alexandra's sister Elizabeth, who had married the Tsar's uncle, Grand Duke Serge. Vyrubova was a young girl when they met. She had been ill, and the Empress, always solicitous of those who were ill, had come on a neighborly visit. From then on, the younger woman showed a dogged devotion to the Empress.

That Vyrubova was of limited intelligence most contemporaries agree. Count Grabbe, among others, found her mean-spirited and vengeful. Baroness Buxhoeveden, who tacitly disapproved of her friendship with the Empress, describes her as a "handsome woman in the florid style" and adds that the Empress found her "unpretentious and guileless." The lady-in-waiting notes however, that Vyrubova "unwittingly harmed the Empress in the later years" by receiving questionable petitioners in her home.

Vyrubova, as Alexandra's confidante, eventually lived in a cottage on palace grounds and had free access to the palace although she didn't have any official court function. She acted as go-between for the Empress and Rasputin. No doubt Vyrubova's faith in Rasputin strengthened her bond with the Empress. Baroness Buxhoeveden states flatly that only Vyrubova and the Empress believed in him. "From her [the Empress's] intense love for her son," the lady-in-waiting concludes, "grew her faith in Rasputin the healer."

The correspondence — in English — between Nicholas and Alexandra during World War I discloses that the Empress again and again pressed on the Tsar the advice of "our friend." As knowledge of Rasputin's influence on high-level appointments and on policy decisions seeped out to the public, the monarchy was compromised and the blame focused on Alexandra. She was spoken of as "the German woman" though she was entirely loyal to her adopted country. However, there were valid grounds for suspicion. The capital was filled with German spies assigned to undermine the monarchy, and the entourage of the *starets* Rasputin was questionable to say the least. Once a bottle of Madeira wine among friends had loosened the reprobate's tongue, military secrets confided to him were no longer secret.

When the strains of war shook Russia, Alexandra's obsessive trust in Rasputin and her headlong meddling in affairs of state had disastrous results. Yet her contributions should also be acknowledged. A surprisingly proficient hospital administrator during the war, she was also a dedicated nurse. And when the Bolsheviks held the family captive in Siberia, her religious faith sustained her and gave her family strength to face their ordeal in the spirit of true Christian martyrs.

This 1903 portrait of the Empress by F. A. von Kaulbach was the Tsar's favorite. *Photo Hanfstaengl, Munich*

The Empress on the *Standart*, taken in 1912. In less than a decade
Alexandra Feodorovna had aged markedly.

The Empress on the *Standart* with her brother, Grand Duke Ernest Louis of Hesse-Darmstadt, who came to visit her in Livadia in 1912.

Foreign Minister S. D. Sazonov was suprised when the Grand Duke confided to him during his visit: "The Tsar is a saint and an angel, but he does not know how to deal with her."

Empress Alexandra Feodorovna with Count Fredericks and her
daughters Tatiana and Maria on the *Standart*. In the background is
Dr. Eugene Botkin, the court physician (1912).

The Empress with her daughters Olga and Tatiana called on the wounded, often dressed in the uniforms of Sisters of Mercy, as shown here (Mogilev 1916).

# Tsarevich Alexis

Tsarevich Alexis (1904–1918). Count Grabbe's first pictures of the Tsarevich were taken on the Imperial yacht *Standart* in 1912 during a cruise in Finland. At the time, Alexis was eight years old. As he grew older, Count Grabbe came to know him on a daily basis, especially during the period when the boy was with his father at the Front and in Mogilev.

He observes: "Tsarevich Aleksei Nikolaievich was an extremely handsome boy. He was svelte, elegant, intelligent, and had unusual presence of mind. He possessed, moreover, other winning qualities: a warm, happy disposition, and a generous nature which made him eager to be of help and enabled him quickly to establish rapport with others.

"Despite his easy manner and outgoing personality, the Tsarevich showed a certain firmness of character and independence of mind. At least it was clear that he intensely disliked submitting to the will of others.

"The Imperial family unanimously considered Alexis their favorite, and he responded to his parents' and sisters' love with equal tenderness and affection."

The Tsarevich's illness hung like an ominous cloud over the lives of the Tsar and his family. Since the least bruise or fall could start internal bleeding into the joints, accompanied by excruciating pain, family life centered around Alexis and happy times related to the periods when he was free of the disease. Often one of his sisters stayed close by to prevent him from accidentally bruising himself.

When Pierre Gilliard, a Swiss tutor, had been teaching the daughters of the Tsar for several years, he was invited to join the family at their hunting lodge in Poland. There the Empress asked him to tutor her son. The lessons soon stopped, however, as Alexis suffered a near-fatal hemorrhage from a fall while getting into a boat. Up to that point Gilliard had not known that there was anything seriously wrong with the Tsarevich, so stringent had been the secrecy surrounding his illness.

At long last he extracted the truth from the doctor in attendance. He also learned that the bleeding had unaccountably stopped when the Empress received from the *starets* Rasputin, a telegram that told her not to worry.

When Gilliard first attempted to tutor Alexis, the boy was wild and undisciplined. The tutor had to use various ploys even to get his attention.

Alexis could hardly bear to be corrected. Still, as Gilliard later commented, he had "so many precious gifts it would be unjust to give up hope."

As the kindly Gilliard persevered, he gradually established rapport with his pupil. In his memoirs he reports that Alexis "had very quick wits and a keen and penetrating mind. He sometimes surprised me with questions beyond his years which bore witness to a delicate and intuitive spirit. . . . Under the capricious little creature I had known at first, I discovered a child of a naturally affectionate disposition, sensitive to suffering in others just because he had already suffered so much himself."

Gilliard continued as tutor to the Tsarevich, accompanied him to the Front, to Army Headquarters, and even to Ekaterinburg.

Tsarevich Alexis on the *Standart* (1912)

(*Top Left*) On board the *Standart* the Tsarevich liked to wear the uniform of a sailor of the Russian navy. As shown here, he occasionally showed the strains of his illness (1912).

(*Top Right*) Tsarevich Alexis with the sailor Derevenko, who was assigned to watch over him (1912)

(*Bottom Left*) Alexis and his father (1912)

(*Bottom Right*) Alexis playing shuffleboard (1912)

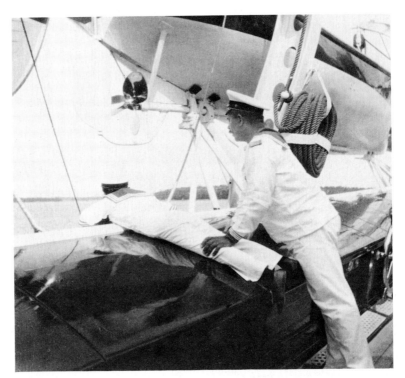

Supported by Derevenko, Alexis looks out to sea, possibly watching the courier bringing the daily mail (1912).

Alexis's cane indicates that the illness has affected his left leg (1912).

While Derevenko (behind, with his own sons) seemed at the time to be patient and conscientious in watching over his charge, his behavior toward Alexis became excessively mean after the Revolution. Fortunately, the boy also had another sailor-attendant, the loyal Nagorny, who stayed with him almost to the very end.

A streak of mischievousness in Alexis's nature shows here as he watches his parents' luncheon guests from behind the palms. "He thoroughly enjoyed life — when it let him," his tutor Gilliard observed, "and was a happy, romping boy." In the foreground is Father Kedrinsky, Court Prelate at the Livadia Palace (1912).

The Tsarevich, Count Grabbe, and Pierre Gilliard during a stop of the Imperial train en route to the Front. Alexis is wearing the uniform of a Russian Army private (1915).

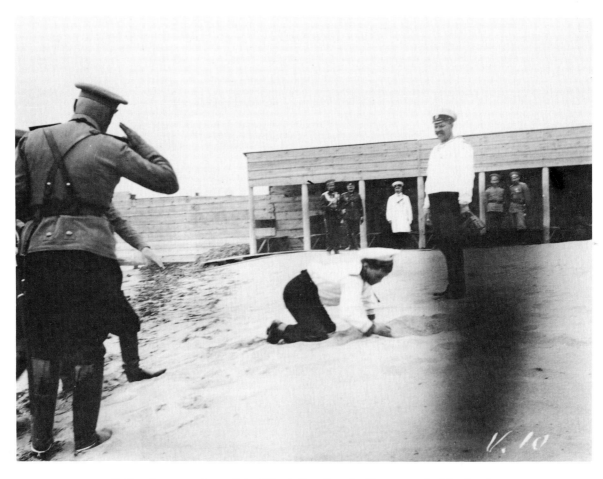

Following a review of the Black Sea fleet in Sevastopol, Alexis plays in the sand. Derevenko hovers protectively nearby (1915).

# The Daughters of the Tsar

The four daughters of the Tsar led an unusually secluded life — seldom seen and seldom photographed. Their personalities, though distinct, were muted by an overcautious and dominating mother steeped in Victorian values. All four were dressed alike and, seen together, looked like identical paper dolls.

The Grand Duchesses, we are told, loved dancing and parties, but their opportunities for fun were limited. Concerned about their monotonous lives, their grandmother, the Dowager Empress Maria Feodorovna, invited them every Sunday to a formal luncheon at her Anitchkov Palace. From there Grand Duchess Olga Alexandrovna, the Tsar's sister, took them to a party in her own home to which were invited a select group of young noblemen and three girl cousins with their mother, the Duchess of Leuchtenberg, as chaperone.

Sometimes the Tsar took the older girls to the theater or ballet in what was then Russia's "Silver Age" of the arts. They seldom went calling in other people's homes and, until the war, knew little of the world outside the palace gates. The family vacations in the Crimea and their cruises on the *Standart* were a welcome change.

"The girls loved the sea," Count Grabbe comments, "and I well remember their joyful anticipation of these cruises on the *Standart*, which opened broader horizons for them, brought them new contacts, and permitted an intimacy with their beloved father which was otherwise impossible. To be at sea with their father — that was what constituted their happiness."

Grand Duchesses Anastasia, Maria, Olga, and Tatiana with Captain Chagine, skipper of the Tsar's yacht, left, and Count Grabbe, who is taking the picture, on the *Standart* (probably 1911).

The Tsar and his daughters — left to right, Olga, Tatiana, Maria, and Anastasia — greet *Standart* officers.

Not yet twelve, Anastasia was already trained like her sisters to carry her handkerchief in her left hand (1912).

## GRAND DUCHESS OLGA NIKOLAIEVNA
### (1895–1918)

Olga, the Tsar's oldest daughter, had glistening blond hair and a fair complexion. Meditative, she sought solitude, enjoyed poetry, and liked to improvise on the piano. Of suitable age, she was the only one to attend balls in St. Petersburg and have royal suitors. In 1914, an attempt to interest her in Crown Prince Carol of Rumania failed. She could be happy married only to a Russian, she told her parents. There was no marriage prospect anywhere in sight, she once sadly confided to Count Grabbe.

"Olga Nikolaievna," says Count Grabbe, "was the most independent of the four daughters. She was quick to grasp an idea and very fond of reading. Olga resembled her father but did not have his reserve." Singularly straightforward in manner, she was said to be "incapable of hiding her soul."

During the war years Olga became aware of the problems facing her father and suffered with him. Objects found in her room in Ekaterinburg after her assassination suggest that she grew in spiritual strength during captivity. Among her belongings was a hymn in her handwriting. It asked the Holy Mother to save Russia and to give her strength to forgive her captors and fortitude to suffer the humiliations forced upon her.

Grand Duchess Olga and Captain Sablin of the *Standart*, a protégé of the Empress (1912)

Olga Nikolaievna during an outing in Mogilev (1916)

During a visit to Kokozy, the Crimean estate of Prince Felix Yussupov, Olga and Tatiana as usual look stately even though their gowns did not come from the Paris couturier Worth, as did their grandmother's. They were made by a St. Petersburg dressmaker patronized by their frugal mother (1912).

# GRAND DUCHESS TATIANA NIKOLAIEVNA
## (1897–1918)

"The prettiest of the Grand Duchesses," says Count Grabbe, "was Tatiana, the Tsar's second daughter. In her physical appearance and her serious and ardent nature, she most resembled her mother.

"She was also the family's manager and organizer, and possessed, more than her sisters, a highly developed sense of her position as the daughter of the Tsar."

Tatiana was very different from Olga in temperament and interests. She was more confident of herself and more reserved, with more perseverance and balance. Slender, with auburn hair and clear gray eyes, she was strikingly good-looking and enjoyed the attention her beauty commanded. As the Empress became more and more an invalid, Tatiana, eighteen months younger than Olga, took over much of the responsibility for the younger children and the household.

Had her life run its natural course, she would have graced many a ball, but with the advent of World War I, Tatiana would instead find herself laboring long hours with her mother and Olga in hospitals caring for the wounded. She was one month short of her twenty-first birthday when she died.

Grand Duchess Tatiana (1912)

Tatiana Nikolaievna with a tennis partner, Count A. Vorontzov-Dashkov, whom she favored. Count Grabbe, seated, acts as chaperone. (Livadia, 1912)

Vyrubova recalls that the Grand Duchesses were "allowed to have a little preference for this or that handsome young officer with whom they danced, played tennis, walked and rode," always properly chaperoned.

Grand Duchess Tatiana, aged sixteen, in a wistful moment on the Finnish coast. Unidentified attendant in background (1913)

# GRAND DUCHESS MARIA NIKOLAIEVNA
## (1899–1918)

Count Grabbe says of the Tsar's third daughter, clearly his favorite: "With her large gray, luminous eyes, her classical features, and languorous movements, she was the true type of Russian beauty, the most good-natured and artless of the four sisters, with endearing qualities which drew people to her."

More outgoing than her older sisters, Maria Nikolaievna loved children and used to talk to soldiers about their families. She knew the names of many of the *Konvoy* Cossacks and *Standart* sailors, took an interest in their affairs and managed out of her $9 a month allowance to send little gifts to their children.

With all her gentle ways, she was strong and solidly built, like her grandfather Alexander III. Her sisters called her "Mashka" and sometimes "Little Bow-wow."

Maria's fun-loving nature is suggested in this picture of her on stilts, taken in Finland (1913).

Maria and Olga on the *Standart* (1912)

Grand Duchesses Maria, left, and Olga during an outing on a Finnish island (1914)

In identical polka-dotted blouses, they show the relaxed mood of a summer excursion out-of-doors. Maria's genial charm is evident, as is Olga's reflective dignity. In the background a sailor carries a stray dog he has just caught, while *Standart* officers and other members of the party look on.

# GRAND DUCHESS ANASTASIA NIKOLAIEVNA
## (1901–1918)

The Tsar's youngest daughter was much the sprightliest and most entertaining. She had a comic gift as a mimic, picking out people's foibles in a way that made everyone laugh. "What a bundle of mischief," recalls her godmother, Grand Duchess Olga Alexandrovna, the Tsar's sister.

There was also a serious side to Anastasia's nature. She had a restless, questioning intelligence. "Whenever I talked with her," says Count Grabbe, "I always came away impressed by the breadth of her interests. That her mind was keenly alive was immediately apparent."

More than her sisters, Anastasia chafed under the narrowness of her environment and used her comic sense in revolt against it.

Despite the persistent rumor that Anastasia survived the murder of her family on the night of July 16/17, 1918, at Ekaterinburg, detailed investigations concluded that she died with her family. When the bullet missed its mark, she is said to have cried out for mercy to the man whose bayonet then ended her life.

An investigation was conducted by a special commission set up by anti-Communist forces shortly after the night of the assassination. Nikolai Sokolov, magistrate of the Omsk tribunal, headed the commission. His report, *Enquête judiciaire sur l'assassinat de la famille impériale russe*, was published in Paris in 1924. A later Soviet probe conducted by P. M. Bykov, president of the Ekaterinburg Soviet, confirmed Sokolov's findings.

However, in the 1920s, a woman named Anna Anderson, who claimed to be Grand Duchess Anastasia, appeared in Germany. A number of Russian émigrés, including Duke George of Leuchtenberg, in whose Bavarian castle she was a guest, supported her claim. The Duke asked Count Grabbe to come and meet the woman in order to give his judgment. Count Grabbe declined. His reason, as he told his family, was that since he had known Anastasia only as a young girl, his judgment could at best be tentative. Yet it would be given undue weight. Anna Anderson later married an American, John Manahan, and came to live in the United States. She died in 1984, her claim still in doubt.

Grand Duchess Anastasia peers down impishly from the deck of the *Standart* (1912).

Anastasia hated the formality of life at court and expressed her protests whenever she could. She even resented the constraint of having a *Konvoy* Cossack assigned to guard her, as this picture suggests (Finland, 1912).

Grand Duchess Anastasia, 15, with her brother, Alexis, 12, near
Mogilev — Count Grabbe's last picture of them (1916)

# Vacationing with the Tsar

## 1912–1914

# *Sojourn in Livadia 1912*

"While in the Crimea," writes Count Grabbe, "the Imperial family stayed at Livadia near Yalta, where all could be together and relatively free from official cares. The Grand Duchesses spoke of it as their real home."

Originally a wooden structure built by Alexander III, Livadia was located on the mountainous coast of the Black Sea. The Empress had had it remodeled in 1911, and it was her special pride. Of white stone in a style she had admired in Italy, the palace became for her a retreat where she could enjoy some peace of mind. And she liked the little white church that adjoined it. The Imperial estate — 800 acres in all — included extensive cultivated parks, gardens, and vineyards — and a panoramic view of the sea.

"Here," says Count Grabbe, "even in the early spring, the nights are incomparable — clear and mild, the air filled with the perfume of flowers. From my balcony I can see the moonlit peaks of the Jaila Range and hear the waves breaking on the rocks below." When the Revolution came, reports Baroness Buxhoeveden, the family hoped they would be allowed to live in Livadia.

"Life in Livadia," Count Grabbe recalls, "was well organized but without any feeling of constraint. In the morning, members of the Tsar's military entourage were usually free to do as they pleased. This was a good time to go for a stroll in Livadia's gardens or go for a swim, or take advantage, as I sometimes did, of the carriage and riding horse assigned to me for my personal use. For lunch, everyone gathered with the Imperial family in the palace dining room. On holidays, a military band played during lunch."

Every Saturday in the late afternoon there was a service in the church that adjoined the palace, and a mass on Sunday morning, followed by a luncheon to which quite a few people from outside Livadia were invited. The Tsar never missed a church service, however tired or indisposed he was.

"On weekdays, after lunch," says Count Grabbe, "the Tsar, the Grand Duchesses, and some members of the Imperial retinue entered automobiles that were waiting for them, and the party set off on long excursions."

The girls enjoyed driving along the coast and through the interior of the Crimea with its colorful native villages, fruit trees in blossom, and vineyard-covered hillsides. Gilliard comments on the dazzling sunshine and the "white mosques standing out against the old cypresses in the Tatar cemeteries."

"The Empress often felt tired and seldom took part in these excursions. Each of the daughters took turns staying with her so she wouldn't be alone," Count Grabbe notes.

Sometimes the Tsar went for long walks. The surrounding mountains, thickly covered with pine trees and shrubs, could be quite precipitous. Ever since he had fallen with his horse while riding there, Nicholas preferred to walk. Count Grabbe recalls that "the Tsar disliked the sight of secret service men posted round and about during these walks. He called them 'nature lovers' because of the concentrated way in which they stared at the sky or the trees, pretending not to see him when he came by. He often tried to give them the slip by unexpectedly changing the direction of his walk. This tug of war eventually developed into a kind of game, each trying to outwit the other."

Social life during the Imperial family's sojourn at Livadia was more lively than at Tsarskoe Selo. Visitors frequently came to lunch. There were picnics, excursions, occasional parties at neighboring estates. As Olga and Tatiana grew older, they were allowed, properly chaperoned, to take part in these activities. A memorable occasion was a ball given at Livadia to celebrate Olga's sixteenth birthday. The Grand Duchess wore her first ball gown and her first jewels, a diamond ring and a diamond necklace, gifts from her parents.

"One day," recounts Count Grabbe, "we boarded the *Standart* and sailed along the coast to visit Novy Svet, the estate of Prince Lev Grigorievich Golitzin. The Prince was internationally known as a pioneer in the development of Russian wines. He lived in a medieval-looking mansion accessible only from the sea along mountain trails. He was, in fact, something of an eccentric, but so colorful and exuberant that the Tsar found him entertaining and liked to talk to him.

"It had amused him to learn that the Prince, to celebrate the fiftieth anniversary of the founding of his winery, had put an advertisement in major Russian newspapers inviting one and all to be his guests at Novy Svet for the festivities."

The Prince's wine cellars, hollowed out of the cliffs, extended about two miles along the coast. There was also a hall carved out of the side of the mountain. Here Prince Golitzin invited his guests to sample some of his wines and entertained them at lunch. "Everyone was delighted with the expedition," says Count Grabbe, "the more so that the Prince never stopped talking and kept everyone amused the whole time." It pleased Prince Golitzin to will his estate and his winery to the Tsar, reports Baroness Sophie Buxhoeveden. However, Nicholas refused because the gift entailed conditions: further development by the government of the wine industry in the area.

Livadia palace and adjoining church (1912)

Livadia's inner court and rose garden was a favorite place for con-
versations after lunch. Marble columns in the center, excavated in
the Crimea, were from ancient times (1912).

The Empress confers with Count Paul Benckendorff, Grand Marshal of the Court, on affairs of the Imperial household. Far left, facing the camera, Anna Vyrubova. Center background, Mme. Narishkin, Mistress of the Robes. Right background, General V. J.
Voyeikov, then Commander of His Majesty's Hussars (1912)

Tatiana and Maria with Count A. Vorontzov-Dashkov. In the background, Anna Vyrubova (1912)

Anastasia on a swing near Livadia palace. Maid of honor, left; *Standart* officer, right (1912)

The Tsar talks with a local military commander in Livadia (1912).

The Tsar and family look out to sea from the terrace of St. George's Convent on the Crimean coast. Grand Duchess Olga in foreground (1912)

The Tsar with daughters during hike near Livadia (1912)

General Doumbadze, Crimean official, the Tsarevich, and a child
visiting the Yussupovs watch across the stream as the Tsar and his
daughters fish for trout during an outing at Kokozy, the Yussupov
estate near Livadia (1912).

The Tsar and Grand Duchesses Tatiana and Maria trout-fishing at Kokozy. At right, in nun's habit, is Grand Duchess Elizabeth, the sister of the Empress, who took the veil when her husband, Grand Duke Serge, was assassinated (1912).

On the Crimean coast the Tsar looks up toward the manor house of Prince Golitzin's estate, Novy Svet, while the *Standart* waits at anchor below (1912).

Prince Golitzin escorts the Tsar around Novy Svet (1912).

The Tsar's party at Novy Svet makes its way back to the launch
which will take them to the *Standart* (1912).

The Tsar (second from left) liked to walk with members of his suite along the shore of the Black Sea — even in stormy weather (1912).

# On Board the Standart

The *Standart* was a graceful seagoing ship, built to the Tsar's own specifications by a Danish shipyard. The size of a small cruiser, it combined elegance and comfort and met all the requirements of a floating palace. Mahogany-paneled quarters spaciously accommodated family, retinue, and guests. Informal wicker furniture on the main deck invited relaxation; awnings overhead shielded the passengers from the sun.

When the Tsar and his family came on board, a large household staff of footmen, stewards, stewardesses, butlers, and cooks attended them. The yacht was manned by a crew from the Imperial Russian Navy. Also on board were a platoon of marines, a brass band, and a balalaika orchestra. The ship was equipped with radio, a novelty in 1912.

"The relationship of the Imperial family to its entourage was very friendly and informal," Count Grabbe recalls. "It was especially cordial with the officers of the *Standart*. These young men were exemplary —

The Tsar's yacht, the *Standart*

charming, modest, possessed of a great deal of dignity and tact, and incapable of any intrigue.

"During cruises, the Tsar often invited these officers to dinner and after the meal liked to play billiards with them or have a game of dominoes. On such occasions the Empress usually sat nearby, sewing, the Tsarevich ran about with his playmates, while the Grand Duchesses, surrounded by all the young men, scattered throughout the yacht. 'We form a united family,' the Empress used to remark while on these voyages."

In his memoirs of court life General Mosolov comments on the childish level of the girls' conversation with the young officers. "I never heard the slightest word or suggestion of the modern flirtation," he says, ". . . even when the two eldest had grown into real young women one might hear them talking like little girls of ten or twelve."

During the summer months preceding World War I, the Allied Powers exchanged official visits to consolidate their alliances. President Poincaré of France came to Russia to call on the Tsar. And Britain, as a gesture of solidarity with Russia, sent to St. Petersburg the First Battle Cruiser Squadron of the Royal Navy under the command of Admiral Sir David Beatty.

Sailors check the rope on one of the lifeboats.

The crew adjusts an awning in preparation for the arrival of the Imperial family.

The Tsar comes on board as Count Benckendorff salutes (1913).

On the *Standart*, the Tsar followed a daily routine. Early each morning he came on deck to check the weather (1913).

He also liked to make the rounds of the ship's company.

The Tsar greets the yacht's warrant officers.
Tsarevich Alexis is wearing a uniform identical to that of the
sailor saluting in left background (1913).

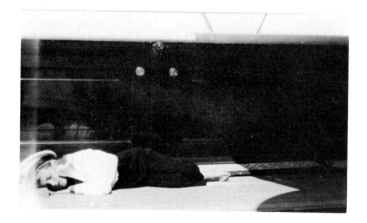

(*Top Left*) The Tsar checks the yacht's course with Captain Zelenet-sky (1913).

(*Top Right*) The Tsar, right, and his Flag Captain, Admiral Nilov (1912)
   Count Grabbe observes that the Tsar was interested in navigation and liked to discuss the subject with his Flag Captain.

(*Bottom*) On sunny afternoons the Tsarevich liked to stretch out on deck.

In *Standart* dining salon: Catherine Schneider (left), who taught
Russian to the Empress and later tutored the girls, and Countess
Anastasia Hendrikov, lady-in-waiting. Alexandra was very fond of
the gentle countess, and often took her along on trips. Both women
followed the Imperial family to Siberia, where they were impris-
oned and later shot by the Bolsheviks (1914).

Front row: Maria, Olga, Alexis, the Tsar, Tatiana, Anastasia
(seated in front), Catherine Schneider, Baroness Buxhoeveden,
Captain Chagine (seated). Count Fredericks is behind Maria, Count
Grabbe at far right.

This picture was taken before a formal sitting. The Grand Duchesses are dressed for the occasion in identical traditional Russian
embroidered linen gowns. Alexis's left leg is turned in, giving evi-
dence of the discomfort caused by his illness. The Tsar seems
amused by what his waggish youngest daughter is saying to Baroness Buxhoeveden, while the girls' tutor, Catherine Schneider, seems
to be bracing herself for what her most irrepressible charge is about
to say (1913).

Grand Duchess Tatiana takes a snapshot of the crew while her
mother and uncle, Grand Duke Ernest Louis of Hesse, look on during his visit in 1912.

The Empress and her daughters on the *Standart* (1912)

Grand Duchess Olga looking pensive (1912)

The Grand Duchesses in the company of the yacht's officers (1913)
Here Olga chats with Admiral Nilov. With her are her sisters,
Maria, who appears to be listening, and Tatiana, who seems to be
more interested in one of the officers than in the conversation.

Anastasia at eleven with the yacht's cutter in background (1912)

The Grand Duchesses Olga, left, and Maria look remarkably plain
yet remarkably pretty in this picture taken during the Imperial family's last cruise on the *Standart* (1914).

Anna Vyrubova on the *Standart* (1914)

On June 20, 1914, the day Count Grabbe records here, Admiral Beatty's imposing gray ships filed past the *Standart* and anchored at Kronstadt. The better to view this smartly executed maneuver, the Tsar with two of his daughters watched from an upper deck of the *Standart*. The Imperial family then went on board HMS *Lion*, the Admiral's flagship, for lunch. After the British left, the Tsar and his family sailed to Finland for their annual vacation. This cruise proved to be very short and turned out to be their last.

Every summer the Tsar and his family vacationed off the coast of Finland. They had found a secluded bay surrounded by small islands, and returned to it year after year. In 1912, when Count Grabbe first accompanied them, he joined the family on the *Standart* at Peterhof and sailed with them to this sheltered anchorage. The Tsar's children had nicknamed it the "Bay of *Standart*."

While visiting their favorite bay, the Tsar and his family lived on the *Standart* but spent a good part of the day on one of the islands. It was uninhabited so that they all felt free to picnic, relax, and enjoy the out-of-doors without fear of being observed by prying eyes.

Except for a tennis court built for the Tsar, arrangements on the island were primitive.

Every day the Imperial family, their retinue, and *Standart* officers boarded the launch and headed for their chosen island (1912).

The Tsar sets out to sea in a kayak, accompanied by Captain Nevi-arovsky of the *Standart*. Of Eskimo origin, the kayak was introduced to Russia from Alaska. As a precaution, two sailors in a rowboat always trailed the Tsar on such expeditions (1912).

The Tsar frequently paddled a distance into the bay, and Count
Grabbe notes that it was difficult to keep up with him (1912).

During his vacation the Tsar was kept free from callers, official and unofficial. An exception was the occasional visit by his mother, the Dowager Empress Maria Feodorovna, who came to the "Bay of *Standart*" in her own beautiful yacht, the *Polar Star*. One such occasion recorded here was the name day of the Dowager Empress and that of her granddaughter Maria, July 22, 1912.

The Dowager Empress, center, on a Finnish island with her granddaughters Tatiana and Anastasia. The Tsar in tennis clothes, left, with Admiral Nilov (1912)

The Dowager Empress Maria Feodorovna, looking remarkably youthful for her age, smiles graciously at the photographer. The Tsar, with his back to the camera, chats with Lieutenant Viazemsky, a naval officer (1912).

Maria Feodorovna with Count Benckendorff, an old friend, who had served her husband, Tsar Alexander III, for a number of years (1912).

Off the Finnish coast, *Standart* officers surround Grand Duchess
Tatiana (not Olga nor 1907 as marked on the negative), who has her
Brownie box camera at her side (1912).

At the end of her visit the Dowager Empress prepares to take her leave.

This picture taken on the *Standart* might be called "The women in his life," and may be the only one in existence showing the Dowager Empress and all the feminine members of the household of Nicholas II.

Shadowy but erect at right is Empress Alexandra Feodorovna with her daughter Olga at her side. In the center stands the Dowager Empress with her back to Alexandra, symbolically enough. "My daughter-in-law does not like me . . . ," she told Count Kokovtzev. Watching from the sidelines is Alexandra's ubiquitous friend, Anna Vyrubova. Others are, left to right, Count Benckendorff, Grand Duchesses Anastasia, Maria, and Tatiana as well as two ladies-in-waiting. An escort destroyer can be seen nearby (1912).

Count Grabbe (third from left) and other spectators watch a tennis game (1912).

The Tsar makes a gesture to Anna Vyrubova by taking her on as tennis partner. *Standart* sailors stand at the end of the court to catch stray balls.

The Tsar looks up quizzically at the horseplay of two *Standart* officers (1912).

Grand Duchess Olga, the Tsar's sister, and her four nieces enjoy the clowning that went on during these informal outings (1912).

The Tsar ruminates as he watches daughters (left to right) Tatiana, Anastasia, and Olga in identical hats and dresses (1913).

Grand Duchess Anastasia, then eleven, in a field of flowers (1912)

The Tsar inspects the destroyer *Voiskovoy* — one of several naval units that escorted the *Standart* or stood guard nearby when he was on board (1913).

The Tsar tastes food from the crew's mess — an essential part of Russian military inspection procedure. Behind him stands Count Grabbe, saluting, and next to him *Voiskovoy*'s skipper and mate (1913).

The Tsar jokes with the skipper and other officers of the *Voiskovoy*.
The *Standart* at anchor in the background (1913)

In mid-July 1914, his brief vacation ended, the Tsar takes one last look at the coast of Finland. It proved, indeed, to be his last look.

When World War I came, the *Standart*, by order of the Tsar, was placed in drydock, and he never again returned to Finnish waters.

# *Visits to the Front*

On August 12, 1914, Russian troops advanced into East Prussia. To the south, another Russian army knocked out the main Austrian force, occupied Galicia, and captured 100,000 prisoners. All too soon the Germans scored a major victory at Tannenberg, but not before they had been forced to withdraw crucial troops from the Battle of the Marne. The Tsar had honored his commitment to France.

The Commander-in-Chief of the Russian armies was the Tsar's tall uncle, Grand Duke Nikolai Nikolaievich. So, when the Tsar visited army headquarters, he was careful not to impinge on his uncle's prerogatives. Nicholas listened attentively to Nikolai Nikolaievich's reports and those of his generals and participated to some extent in military decisions. He did not have enough knowledge of military science to take a more active role.

At the Front it was different. Nicholas was heartened to believe that through contact with his soldiers — inspiring them by his presence and words of praise, distributing decorations among them — he was helping Russia in a tangible way to fight the war.

In the first two years of the war, the Tsar traveled some 50,000 miles in the Imperial Train visiting troops and hospitals in the German, Austrian, and Turkish fronts. Still, he barely glimpsed the terrors of battle since the High Command tried to keep him out of danger zones. His visits to hospitals were the closest he came to observing the ravages of battle. As a result, there was for the Tsar an aura of unreality about the war.

"It is difficult to believe," he wrote to the Empress from army headquarters at Baranovici in October 1914, "that a great war is raging not far from this place; everything seems so peaceful and quiet. The life here reminds me of the old days when we were staying here during maneuvers."

Austrian prisoners taken by the Russians in Galicia prepare for
evacuation (1914).

Caught in a war of movement, Austrian prisoners sometimes had to fend for themselves. Many roamed the Galician countryside looking for food and shelter (1914).

The Tsar inspects a supply train in Poland during one of his first
visits to the Front. With him are, left to right, General Voyeikov
and Colonel Mordvinov (October 1914).

An Army unit in Poland awaits the Tsar's arrival in October 1914.

Officers to be decorated form a square. The Tsar is at center, with aide carrying decorations following him. Behind the aide is Grand Duke Nikolai Nikolaievich (1914).

On December 14, 1914, the Tsar telegraphed the Empress: "Have spent an ever-memorable day . . . right on the [Turkish] frontier. There were collected all the lower ranks of the Caucasian Army who had most distinguished themselves, about 1,200 men. I distributed crosses and medals of St. George among them; they had come straight from the advanced positions and had an excellent sunburnt appearance." Here the Tsar reviews the men to be decorated for bravery and then distributes the medals.

Bleak landscape of the Galician battle zone (1914)

In the spring of 1915, the Tsar visited Przemysl, a major Austrian fortress captured by the Russians. He insisted on going there despite the reservations of the High Command, who considered the area a danger zone. The fortress was in fact retaken six weeks later. Here, the Tsar climbs over the destroyed ramparts of Przemysl.

Austrian prisoners gaze at the Tsar's party as it goes by (1915).

128

Imperial train waits while Court dignitaries confer with local officials.

The Imperial train was a glistening deep blue and had a small gold monogram — N II — on its doors. The Tsar used it on various trips to the Front. Prior to the war, it served mainly for the long journey to the Crimea.

Travel arrangements for the Imperial train were extensive. The railroad administration had to arrange routes, alternate routes, and time schedules; the War Ministry had to be notified so that sentries could be posted near bridges and tunnels; the Ministry of the Interior informed as well as governors of provinces through which the train would pass.

Still other preparations were needed when the Tsar traveled by train. A trunkful of assorted presents for him to distribute — goblets, cigarette cases, engraved boxes — had to be selected and packed. On trips to the Front, decorations for the soldiers were included. The office of the Marshal of the Court had to be advised so that accommodations could be prepared in advance for the Tsar and his entourage. Last, the palace police and the secret service had to be given a detailed itinerary.

The train had eight cars. Next to the locomotive was the car that carried a complement of *Konvoy* Cossacks. When the train stopped at a station, four Cossacks took up guard duty on the station platform outside the Tsar's quarters. The second car housed the kitchen and kitchen staff. The third car, a diner, seated sixteen. At one end was a small drawing room with a piano. The Tsar was delighted to have the diner so close to the kitchen. Then he could be served his food when it was still hot, an amenity he seldom enjoyed at the palace. Count Grabbe recalls that in appreciation he frequently complimented the chef.

The Tsar and Empress occupied the fourth car, which included the Tsar's study, furnished with a desk and green leather armchairs; their bedroom; bath and a boudoir decorated in gray and lilac, the Empress's favorite color. An outside corridor permitted other passengers to go by without disturbing Their Majesties.

The fifth car carried the children and ladies-in-waiting. The sixth car was reserved for the Tsar's suite and had a compartment, usually unoccupied, reserved for local dignitaries, such as governors of provinces, who sometimes boarded the train to confer with the Tsar and might stay overnight. The seventh car was for baggage. In the eighth and final car traveled Chancellery and Military Secretariat staffs, the Court physician, whose compartment adjoined a dispensary, the domestic staff, and the train commandant.

Curiously enough, the train had a duplicate, which was outwardly identical. As a precaution, one traveled ahead of the other and no one was told, not even the railroad administration, which one came first.

Imperial family greets civil servants in Feodosia, a Crimean seaport (1915).

In the dining car of the Imperial train en route to the front lines
(1915)
    Clockwise: Count Grabbe, Count Fredericks, Count Shereme-
tiev, Captain Sablin, Grand Duke Dimitri Pavlovich, the Tsar,
Tsarevich Alexis, and General Voyeikov. The Tsar is on his way to
Rovno, then in southern Poland. From there, he went another
twelve miles by car to visit troops close to the German lines.

The Tsar goes for a stroll before reviewing the Black Sea fleet.
With him are, left to right, Grand Duchesses Anastasia, Tatiana,
Maria, Olga, Tsarevich Alexis, Prince Igor Konstantinovich, Ro-
manov kin. A crowd watches from the hillside.

The Tsar's daughters in Sevastopol: left to right Tatiana, Olga, Anastasia, Maria. In the shadow of a window at the extreme left, the ever-shy Empress

Grand Duchess Anastasia beside the Imperial train at Sevastopol. A naval ferry in the background

The trip "did everyone good," recalled Baroness Buxhoeveden, who accompanied the Empress. Olga and Tatiana needed a change after nursing the wounded. Olga had grown nervous and anemic. All four daughters "used to lie like lizards in the sun beside the train" at Sevastopol.

The Tsar on a cruiser talks with Admiral N. O. Essen. It was said of this hard-bitten seadog that when the Tsar, momentarily forgetting that a war was on, radioed the fleet at sea, "Where are you?" the Admiral wryly replied, "I don't know."

Tatiana stands near her brother, taking her turn at his side in case he should lose his balance.

The Tsar's party, in a naval launch, returns from a cruiser to Sevastopol.

The Grand Duchesses at the hospital in Yevpatoria in the Crimea.
In the left background are wounded men they have come to see.
The tall lady in the center is Rita Hitrovo, Olga's lady-in-waiting
(1915).

The Empress, in a white hat, and Grand Duchess Olga on their
way to a hospital in western Ukraine in the Delaunay-Belleville, the
Tsar's favorite car (1915)

While the Tsar traveled to the fronts bolstering the troops, the Empress
worked indefatigably visiting and caring for the wounded. Long before
World War I, the Empress had concerned herself with hospital care in
Russia, to which she brought a knowledge of English practices. She looked
on hospital work as a mission, and when war came she used her organizing
ability to institute a system of hospital and sanitary trains that extended
as far south as Odessa.

With her two older daughters, Alexandra enrolled in a nursing course
taught by a woman surgeon. All three earned diplomas as full-fledged
nurses. Engrossed in her work as a nurse, the Empress seemed to forget
her physical ills as she labored long hours to comfort the wounded and
assisted in the operating room even with the most serious casualties.

In May 1915 the Germans, in a shift of strategy, decided to dispose of

Russia before Italy had a chance to attack Austria. They massed 161 divisions and all available artillery on the Eastern Front. Przemysl fell June 3. Throughout the summer the Germans advanced. Warsaw fell August 4; Vilna, September 18. By then the offensive had spent itself, yet victory eluded the Germans. Though they were now secure enough to shift their forces to the Western Front, the Russian Army, while badly battered, was still extant.

From May to September the Tsar watched in dismay the retreat of his armies, the mounting casualties. He had felt other pressures: demands for a more responsible government, new Army leadership. In addition, the Empress persistently urged him to replace Nikolai Nikolaievich. The Grand Duke, she thought, overshadowed her husband.

On August 21, 1915, eight ministers signed a letter to the Tsar imploring him not to dismiss Grand Duke Nikolai Nikolaievich and not to assume the high command. "Your decision," it ran in part, "threatens with serious consequences Russia, your dynasty, and your person." They would pay for their candor.

Despite the appeal of the majority of his cabinet, Nicholas dismissed the Grand Duke and took over the High Command. He then moved to Mogilev, provincial capital in western Russia, to which General Headquarters had been transferred.

Tall, soldierly, popular with the troops, Grand Duke Nikolai Nikolaievich, Supreme Commander of the Russian Army during the
first year of the war. He is seen here at Baranovichi, near his train,
from which he directed operations (1915).

Count Fredericks and Tsarevich Alexis stand with Grand Duke
Dimitri Pavlovich, cousin of the Tsar, in front of the Imperial train.
The Grand Duke took part in Rasputin's murder the following
year. Shortly after this picture was taken Alexis had a near-fatal attack and had to be rushed to Tsarskoe (1915).

# *Army Headquarters at Mogilev*

In Mogilev the Tsar took up residence in two rooms of the governor's mansion. Relieved to be a part of Army life again, he instituted a simple routine. Mornings he spent at army headquarters listening to reports from field commanders and discussing military operations with General Alekseiev, his Chief of Staff.

Count Grabbe's notes and photographs give little indication of the Tsar's role at headquarters in making military decisions. They focus, rather, on leisure-time activities in which he himself took part.

So we are told that at one o'clock the Tsar stopped working and was joined for lunch by members of his suite, the heads of the Allied military missions, and possibly a guest or two. After lunch he worked until about three and then exercised out-of-doors. He particularly enjoyed rowing down the river or exploring country roads.

After supper he often played dominoes with members of his suite. The rest of the evening he spent reading dispatches from the Front and studying reports from the capital. He seldom retired before 1:30 A.M.

Frequently the Tsar drove into the country, left his retinue and his car, a Delauney-Belleville, and walked with one or two aides to some remote spot where he sought solitude in natural surroundings. On such occasions, Count Grabbe recalls, he discouraged all conversation.

After he had been at general headquarters for a time, the Tsar brought his son to Mogilev, and in mid-December 1915 took him to review regiments stationed in Galicia. En route Alexis caught a cold. Sneezing brought on a nosebleed, which could not be stopped.

"During the night," reports Gilliard, "the boy got worse. His temperature had gone up and he was getting weaker. At three o'clock in the morning [Dr.] Feodorov, alarmed at his responsibilities, decided to have the Tsar roused and ask him to return to Mogilev. . . . But the boy's state was so alarming that it was decided to take him back to Tsarskoe Selo. . . . The patient's strength was failing rapidly" due to loss of blood. "Twice in the night," recalls the tutor, "he swooned away and I thought the end had come."

In Tsarskoe Selo, however, "the doctors ultimately succeeded in cauterizing the scar which had formed at the spot where a little blood vessel had burst. Once more the Tsarina attributed the improvement in her son's condition to the prayers of Rasputin, and she remained convinced that the boy had been saved thanks to his intervention."

It was February before the Tsarevich was strong again and several months before his mother allowed him to return to General Headquarters.

In background, the governor's mansion, residence of the Tsar in Mogilev. The Cossack sentry in foreground guards army headquarters (1915).

The Tsar on the bank of the Dnieper (spring 1916)

The Tsar liked to stand at this spot on the Dnieper gazing at a distant church. He often returned here when he felt strained; it seemed to calm him, Count Grabbe reports (1916).

Early in 1916 the war situation looked brighter for the Russians. In February they had scored a major victory over the Turks by capturing the fortress of Erzurum, and in the late spring General Brusilov launched his successful offensive in Galicia.

By that time munitions were getting through to the troops and the British had promised delivery of much-needed rifles. However, conditions on the home front continued to be a source of worry for the Tsar.

Russia had called to the colors all available manpower — 15,000,000 men — more soldiers than it could use or even equip. Millions of these conscripts were stationed in the rear, far from the fighting, unproductive and costly to maintain. They were a drain on the economy and a ready target for revolutionary propaganda.

The withdrawal of so many workers from factories and farming areas affected production and food supplies, exacerbating other economic ills: shrinking revenues, a soaring cost of living, overburdened railroads, food and fuel shortages in the cities. Periodically the Tsar's ministers reported on these problems to him.

Even more troubling for the Tsar was the political situation. In the forefront of those who spoke out for change were the leaders of the zemstvos and municipalities who had formed a national organization to help the government care for the wounded and expedite the war effort. In the Duma, too, there was renewed pressure. Political parties of the center, uniting in a Progressive bloc, demanded a government they could trust. They were at one in this respect with educated opinion.

In February 1916, Sir George Buchanan, the British Ambassador, made the first of several courageous attempts "to induce the Emperor to steer a more liberal course." He told the Tsar that officers and even generals who had returned from the Front were calling for a clean sweep. Sir George was so bold as to add that the sacrifices of the Russian people merited consideration. His assignment was to keep Russia in the war at all costs. Recent ministerial appointments were cause of particular concern.

Others managed to reach Nicholas to urge constitutional reform, but all in vain. Discussion of any changes, he invariably said, must be deferred until after the war.

The Tsar wanted his son back with him as soon as Alexis recovered from his latest illness. The masculine atmosphere of army headquarters was good for the boy, he remarked. And so, in May 1916, the Tsarevich and his tutor, Pierre Gilliard, came back to Mogilev. Lessons were resumed on a little veranda in the governor's mansion. Afternoons, says Gilliard, they sometimes sailed on the Dnieper in a small yacht; several times a week they went walking with the Tsar and some of his aides.

As space in the governor's mansion was limited, Alexis slept on a cot in the Tsar's bedroom. He also saw his father at meals. Lunch was his favorite, for then he met a variety of front-line officers and got to know the heads of the Allied military missions. He grew especially fond of the British representative, General Sir John Hanbury-Williams, and the Belgian general, Baron B. de Ricquel, whom he called "Papa Ricquel."

Hanbury-Williams recalls that "in the periods of what may be called his good health, he had all the spirits and the mischief of any ordinary boy of his age."

"As time went on and his first shyness wore off," says Hanbury-Williams, "he [Alexis] treated us as friends and . . . had always some fun with us. With me it was to make sure that each button of my coat was properly fastened, a habit which naturally made me take great care to have one or two unbuttoned, in which case he used at once to stop and tell me I was 'untidy again.'

"In a small alcove adjoining the dining room, every conceivable game went on, a 'rag' in fact, ending most likely in a game of football with anything that came handy . . . and it generally ended by the intervention of the Emperor, by which time the small boy was carefully hidden behind a curtain."

Later that year, when Sir John received news of his oldest son's death in France, he was comforted by the Tsarevich. He reports that before dinner that night he was sitting alone in an anteroom next to the Emperor's quarters when Alexis "came out of his father's room, ran up to me and sat next me, saying: 'Papa told me to come to sit with you as he thought you would feel lonely tonight.'"

Lessons with Gilliard went on after a fashion, but the tutor found the atmosphere at headquarters too stimulating for Alexis, bad for his health; it distracted him from his studies. At times he had to be disciplined. The Tsar seemed mutely to disapprove. So, getting no help from the father, Gilliard decided it was time to take a long-deferred vacation.

At the capital, where he went for a few weeks of rest in July 1916, Gilliard was summoned to Tsarskoe by the Empress and had a long talk with her. She agreed with everything the tutor told her but insisted that her son stay in Mogilev.

"With a candor that utterly amazed me," says Gilliard, "she said that all his life the Tsar had suffered terribly from his natural timidity and from the fact that as he had been kept too much in the background, he had found himself badly prepared for the duties of a ruler. . . . [He] had vowed to avoid the same mistakes in the education of his son."

The decision that Alexis should stay in Mogilev, Gilliard realized, could not be reversed. It was agreed, though, that the lessons should continue and that the tutor receive some help.

The Tsarevich gave Gilliard such an affectionate welcome when he returned to Mogilev the tutor congratulated himself on the wisdom of leaving his pupil for a time. Lessons were resumed with the assistance of English and Russian tutors.

So touching are the Tsar's expressions of affection for his son in letters to Alexandra that it is surprising to learn from Gilliard that once or twice when he was under strain "he spoke roughly to Alexis Nicolaievitch."

A pause for Alexis to rest during hike near Mogilev (1916)
  Left to right: Pierre Gilliard, Count Sheremetiev, Dr. Feodorov,
Prince Dolgoruky, Count Grabbe, the Tsar, Tsarevich Alexis, and
Prince Igor Konstantinovich

The Tsar with the military attachés of the Allied Powers. Left to right: General Sir John Hanbury-Williams, Great Britain; the Tsar; General Baron B. de Ricquel, Belgium; General Janin, France; Colonel Marsengo, Italy (1916)

The Tsar and his party walk along the left bank of the Dnieper in the environs of Mogilev. An old-fashioned paddle steamer plods upstream (1916).

At breakfast in Mogilev: the Tsar, Tsarevich Alexis, Count
Grabbe, and *Fligel Adjutant* Count Sheremetiev reading a report
from the Front (1916)

During the summer and fall of 1916 the Empress and her four daughters
came several times to Mogilev. Military commanders looked askance at
these visits. Totally ignoring them, Alexandra returned again and again to
see her son and her husband and also to lobby for some candidate or
policy. On these occasions the Empress and her daughters lived in the
Imperial train and stayed about a week each time.

When they came, an effort was made to plan excursions and picnics
into the countryside so that everyone could relax from the strains of war.
Sometimes even the Empress came along.

"The Grand Duchesses loved coming to Mogilev," says Count Grabbe.
"The trips enabled them not only to escape briefly from their cloistered
existence and be with their father but provided opportunities for meeting
attractive officers; and for Olga and Tatiana the visits came as a welcome
respite from the many tiring hours spent at Tsarskoe Selo taking care of
the wounded and assisting at operations at the military hospital the Empress had set up there."

Tsarevich Alexis with his sisters Olga, left, and Tatiana during a family outing in Mogilev

During this period Alexis seems to have been free from bruises severe enough to cause a recurrence of his illness. However, his leg must still have bothered him, as we can infer from the cautious way he lowers himself to the deck (1916).

The Grand Duchesses look down playfully from a window of the governor's mansion (1916).

Left to right, Count Grabbe, Grand Duchess Maria, the Tsar, Grand Duchesses Tatiana and Anastasia, *Fligel Adjutant* Mordvinov, and Grand Duchess Olga on a hike near the Dnieper (1916). The Tsar's daughters were well aware of their father's habit of taking strenuous hikes. Undeterred, they put on high boots and came along.

*Fligel Adjutant* Mordvinov with the Grand Duchesses: left to right,
Maria, Anastasia, Tatiana, and Olga (1916)

The Tsar looks particularly jaunty as he chats with Countess Hendrikov. The Empress is in a white blouse. In the background, officers of the suite and Anastasia, whose stance suggests a growing independence in manner and dress (1916)

Among the most informal shots taken by Count Grabbe are those of the Tsar's daughters relaxing in the summer sun at Mogilev (1916).

The Tsar's daughters resting near a haystack. With them is Count Grabbe, who took the picture (1916).

Anastasia, far left, may be pretending to smoke a cigarette (1916).

During a picnic, the Empress, far right, relaxes under a tree while
the Tsar, with his back to the camera, talks to his daughters (1916).

On a walk, the Tsar and Olga survey the river from a hill (1916).

In the summer the Grand Duchesses wore white and, as usual, their dresses were identical. Tatiana and Maria are at right, Anastasia behind Olga. Members of the suite and a lady-in-waiting are in the background.

On a haystack during an outing near Mogilev: left to right, Count
Grabbe taking the picture; the Tsar; behind them, Colonel Mordvinov; next to the Tsar, Grand Duchess Maria; behind her, Grand
Duchess Anastasia, lady-in-waiting (probably Baroness Buxhoeveden), Grand Duchess Olga.

Even on a family outing the mood is no longer cheerful, and
Olga, perhaps the most perceptive of the daughters, here seems def-
initely depressed (1916).

The Tsarevich, aged 12, with his sisters Olga, left, and Tatiana. Flanking Alexis are two military school cadets brought in to be his playmates.

The military school cadets who were invited from time to time to keep the Tsarevich company were much too much in awe of him, says Count Grabbe, to provide real companionship.

In an off moment the Tsar shows his feelings during a boat ride with his daughter. Even the usually jovial Grand Duchess Maria here appears to look grim (1916).

The last three pictures in this sequence suggest that the Tsar and his children were already gravely concerned about the future.

# Rasputin Must Go

The most intractable of the Tsar's problems long had been the dissolute peasant known as Rasputin. His influence over the Empress was more embarrassing to Nicholas than the latter could admit. This improbable Siberian adventurer had not only managed to convince Alexandra Feodorovna that he alone could ease her son's suffering; he had even led her to believe he was a man of God with access to the Almighty. His importance to the Imperial family had been hushed up for years, but by 1916 he was widely recognized as a political liability.

There still may be argument as to whether Gregory Rasputin was an out-and-out scoundrel or merely a libertine tempted by power. What has never been disputed was his peculiar impact on all who saw him.

"It was a gray, windy day of April in the year 1916," reports Meriel Buchanan, daughter of the British Ambassador, "and a heavy fall of snow . . . had made the street almost impassable. . . . An *izvoschik* [horse-drawn cab], drawn by a shaggy white horse . . . had to stop abruptly just in front of where I was standing.

"In the *izvoschik* sat a tall, black-bearded man with a fur cap drawn down over long straggling hair, a bright blue blouse, and long high-boots showing under his fur-trimmed overcoat. Pale gray, deep-set but amazingly brilliant eyes were looking at me, and while that gaze held me I stood motionless . . . held by a sensation of helplessness. . . . Then . . . the driver . . . flicked his horse with his bright green reins and forged on ahead, shouting to the carts to make way for him.

"With his going a weight of repression seemed lifted from me and I gave a quick sigh of relief, shaking myself a little as if with that movement I could rid myself of something disturbing and repellent." From a conversation between two women standing nearby, Miss Buchanan realized who was in the *izvoschik*.

According to S. P. Beletsky, director of the police department in Petrograd, Rasputin was a complex person. A man of powerful physique, he was "at one and the same time ignorant and eloquent, virtuous and sinful, ascetic and a *débauché*, and always a spellbinder."

The British historian Richard Charques speaks of his "possessing unusual peasant shrewdness and a histrionic sense that eventually enabled him to effect hypnotic powers."

159

Gregory Rasputin (1872–1916)

*Historical Picture Service*

Count Grabbe recalls seeing Rasputin only once, at the railroad station in Tsarskoe Selo, when the man was pointed out to him from a distance.

Gregory Rasputin began his life in the remote Siberian village of Pokrovskoye, where he early became aware of his personal magnetism and decided to make his way in the world as a religious pilgrim. With some knowledge of church liturgy picked up at a nearby monastery and some powers as a healer, he set out as a Man of God. When he reached St. Petersburg, church dignitaries sponsored him — much to their later regret. In this way he penetrated some salons and people began to call him *starets*, the Russian term for "venerable older man of saintly habits." Soon he met two mystically inclined Montenegrin princesses married to Russian grand dukes. With the thought that he might heal the new heir's hemophilia, they hastened to introduce Rasputin to the Empress.

At that time little was known about hemophilia. Only in the 1960s was it found that relaxation of tension can reduce, even stop, bleeding. It may be that the hemorrhaging of the Tsarevich stopped because Alexandra's faith in Rasputin's prayers calmed her. Then her son, in turn, relaxed. Baroness Buxhoeveden tartly observes that Gregory "always managed to come when there was a tendency to improvement."

For reasons of public relations Rasputin's appearance at the palace was discouraged. Anna Vyrubova, who saw the *starets* as a miracle healer, carried messages back and forth.

Grand Duchess Tatiana and Anna Vyrubova (1914)

Rasputin was no Man of God. He was a libertine who took advantage of Alexandra's belief in him. He indulged in the most extravagant carousals and drunken sprees, and was an exhibitionist as well. Even society women responded to his dogma that through sin comes redemption. At the same time he was careful to keep his lecherous exploits from the Empress and from her companion Vyrubova. To them he presented himself as a simple *muzhik*, the voice of the peasantry.

When any official attempted to report Rasputin's scandalous behavior to the Tsar, he listened and did nothing. Anyone even remotely critical of Rasputin suffered Alexandra's displeasure. So it happened to Count Grabbe.

As he describes the sequence of events: "In the fall of 1914, the Empress learned of the ailment of my son, Georges, who was mentally retarded, and suggested to me through an intermediary that it might be well for me to meet Rasputin and ask his help. Although aware of the likely consequences of a refusal, I declined to see the *starets*. There was an immediate cooling in my relationship with the Empress."

The Empress, Count Grabbe, and Grand Duchess Olga during an outing on the Dnieper (1916)

Although the Empress was already trying to persuade the Tsar to transfer Count Grabbe elsewhere, on the surface there was no apparent change in their relationship.

Then came a train derailment in which Vyrubova was seriously injured. She was pulled from the wreckage by a sergeant of the *Konvoy* under Count Grabbe's command. On her recovery, Vyrubova demanded that he promote her rescuer. He explained that soldiers could not be promoted because of someone's gratitude, but she insisted. "Finally there was an open quarrel," Count Grabbe writes, "and she announced to me: 'If that's the way it is, you'll see!' I did not have long to wait."

Correspondence between the Tsar and his wife tells how Vyrubova got her revenge. Mogilev had a tennis club frequented by the glamorous wife of an officer. Well aware of Alexandra's jealous nature, Vyrubova told the Empress that Count Grabbe was encouraging the Tsar to visit the club as a pretext to bring him and the lady together. Though this was fabrication, Alexandra Feodorovna believed every word of it. "You may be quite sure," the Tsar wrote her, "that I shall *not make her acquaintance.* . . . But you, for your part must not allow A. [Anna Vyrubova] to bother you with stupid tale-bearing — that will do no good, either to yourself or to others."

However, it was not long before the Tsar offered Count Grabbe an appointment as Ataman of the Don. "From that day," he recounts, "knowing how things are run at Court, I began planning for early retirement."

When Rasputin first met the Empress he asked nothing for himself. Then as news of his influence with the Imperial family spread, people from many walks of life began to make tracks to his door. All sought favors. Some brought money, in which he was actually not interested. Many brought gifts. Some of the prettier petitioners had occasion to dash screaming from his apartment to report to the police an attempted rape. Still, a note from Rasputin brought results and the police were impotent.

Petitioners were not the only people who congregated around Rasputin's apartment. In his camarilla were a questionable foreign banker and at least one German spy. The place swarmed with policemen and plainclothesmen whose assignment it was not only to protect the *starets* in case anyone tried to do him harm, but to take detailed notes on Rasputin's visitors and the reason for their coming. At first the *starets* objected to this surveillance, but after a while he developed friendly relations with the policemen, who greeted him and tipped their hats when he appeared. On occasion they were able to be of service to him.

In one instance, two irate husbands stormed into the building brandishing revolvers and shouting that they knew their wives were with Rasputin and that they planned to avenge their honor. While one of the detectives barred the way, another raced up the stairs to warn Rasputin, who managed to hurry the wives down the backstairs before the husbands burst in through the front door.

The Tsar with his children and *Konvoy* officers in Mogilev on the anniversary in October, 1916, of the *Konvoy* regiment commanded by Count Grabbe. This picture preceded an official photograph. The Imperial family are, left to right, Grand Duchess Anastasia, Olga, the Tsar, the Tsarevich, Grand Duchess Tatiana and behind her, Maria. Count Grabbe stands behind Anastasia.

Barely had the Tsar left for Mogilev in the fall of 1915 to assume military command than the Empress began to take a more active part in national affairs. Once parted from her husband, she grew anxious lest persons hostile to autocracy might influence him. Be firm, she wrote, "proving yourself the autocrat without which Russia cannot exist." Every day she sent him a letter — many peppered with Rasputin's advice and admonitions.

The Tsar, far from reproving his wife, encouraged her. "Yes, truly, you ought to be my eyes and ears there at the capital." In thus encouraging his wife to govern in his place, historians point out, the Tsar was following an old tradition of the great princes of Muscovy, who looked on their lands as family domains and expected their consorts to rule when they went off to war.

When the Tsar's ministers urged him to remain in the capital and not assume supreme command, the Empress, indignant at what she saw as insubordination, pressured the Tsar to dismiss these men. Within a year they were all gone.

In 1916 alone, seventeen ministers were dismissed — an unprecedented turnover of top government officials. In many instances these ministers were replaced by lesser men chosen or approved by Rasputin. Even the Tsar protested to his wife that so many changes were unsettling to the country. In spite of this protest and growing public concern, Rasputin's influence increased. It affected not only ministerial appointment, but also military decisions. For example, when General Brusilov was making a successful advance into Galicia, Rasputin was able to halt the offensive with the argument that too much blood was being spilt.

One of the worst appointments was that of a Rasputin protégé, B. V. Stürmer, as premier early in 1916. The French ambassador, Maurice Paléologue, describes him as a man of "mean spirit, low character, and doubtful honesty." When the Tsar charged the foreign minister, S. D. Sazonov, to draft a manifesto proclaiming Polish autonomy, ostensibly to further Polish cooperation in the war, Stürmer maneuvered to cancel this action. To Sazonov's surprise, he received a note of dismissal. Stürmer had dissuaded the Tsar and the Empress had made a special trip to Mogilev to back up Stürmer.

That visit was probably the occasion on which Vyrubova overheard hostile comments about the Empress at a garden party. In her memoirs she quotes an officer of a foreign military mission remarking, "'She has come again it appears to see her husband and give him the latest orders of Rasputin.'"

"In November 1916," writes Count Grabbe, "public excitement against 'the powers of darkness' supported by the Empress reached a climax."

Alarmed at what they heard, several persons with access to the Tsar spoke to him of the peril to the monarchy. Warnings came from the Dowager Empress, from Grand Duke Nikolai Mikhailovich, respected historian and cousin of the Tsar, from the field chaplain at headquarters, Father Shavelsky. The Empress, they said, must be curbed, Rasputin banished. More warnings would come from the leaders of the nobility, other members of the Romanov family, the British Ambassador, the president of the Duma, M. V. Rodzianko.

Gracious as ever, the Tsar listened, but did nothing. By this time even the staunchest monarchists had decided that Rasputin must go. Some looked on his removal as a patriotic mission.

Count Grabbe notes an extraordinary event that occurred on the night of December 30: "Gregory Rasputin was killed in Petrograd at the home of Prince Yussupov. In Mogilev only the Tsar, Count Fredericks, and Voyeikov knew about it. The rest of us suspected nothing, though *Fligel Adjutant* Mordvinov and I observed that the Tsar was in especially high spirits when he went for a walk. He whistled and hummed, apparently pleased. . . .

During a walk on the afternoon of the day when he learned of Rasputin's murder, "the Tsar," Count Grabbe reports, "was in especially high spirits" (December 31, 1916). Shortly thereafter, the Tsar left for Tsarskoe Selo.

"The next day we started out for Tsarskoe, and only in the train did we learn about the murder. Then the reason for the Tsar's good humor the previous day became clear: he now felt free from a terrible burden."

The Tsar stayed at Tsarskoe Selo two months. Among the few people he saw was Grand Duke Alexander Mikhailovich, his brother-in-law, who burst in with an impassioned plea for a responsible government, accusing Alexandra of dragging down the monarchy. The Tsar quietly escorted him from the room. Another visitor, former Premier Kokovtsev, was shocked by the Tsar's haggard appearance. So was the French Ambassador, who concluded that Nicholas was "now resigned to disaster."

Unexpectedly, at General Alekseiev's urging, the Tsar left for Mogilev on March 8, 1917, though he was needed at the capital. The next day, his children came down with measles. If they had become ill twenty-four hours earlier, he might not have gone. Who can say, then, what might have happened?

"At the Yacht Club, where I had some business," relates Count Grabbe, "club members, on hearing that I was returning to general headquarters with the Tsar, acted as if I were setting forth on some perilous journey.

"When we left Tsarskoe that afternoon, it was without the Tsarevich. This happened to be our last trip to army headquarters."

Mikhailovsky Square, in the center of Petrograd. Within days of the Tsar's return to Mogilev on March 8, 1917, revolutionary crowds would fill the square. (Postcard of the period)

# The Final Days

Even as the Tsar left Tsarskoe there were signs of trouble at the capital. A snag in the distribution of flour had started a rumor that bread was short. Immediately there was a run on bakeries. The same day, the giant Putilov metal works in Petrograd closed in a wage dispute. In retaliation its 30,000 workers went on strike. Adding to other miseries, the temperature had begun to drop. As thousands queued up to wait for bread, the freezing cold increased their anger and frustration.

From headquarters Count Grabbe notes in his diary for March 10, 1917, "We reach Mogilev safely and everything seems quiet here. The Tsar resumes his daily routine."

Meanwhile, authorities in Petrograd were sending optimistic reports to the Tsar, leading him to believe that the ferment in the capital could be handled by the police. Later that day, a telephone call from A. I. Spiridovich, head of Tsarskoe palace security, told a different story: 250,000 workers on strike . . . unrest spreading . . . large crowds singing revolutionary songs gathered around the center of town . . . some bakeries sacked, cars overturned . . . no shots fired as yet.

On hearing this report, the Tsar wired General Khabalov, military commander at the capital, to put an end to the disorders at once.

*Sunday, March 11, 1917.* "During mass at the cathedral," notes Count Grabbe, "the Tsar had a tired and worried look." As later became known, Nicholas wrote his wife that during the service he had suffered "an excruciating pain in the chest. I could hardly stand the service out, and my forehead was covered with drops of perspiration . . . ." Symptoms of a heart attack.

*Monday, March 12, 1917,* was the first day of the Revolution. In Petrograd life had come to a standstill. Banks, schools, factories were closed. Streetcars were not running. Excited crowds milled about. Here and there street fighting had erupted. Several police stations were burning.

Some units of the Volynsky regiment — mostly raw recruits — mutinied. They rushed out of their barracks to join the crowd. News of their defection spread rapidly, precipitating other mutinies. From the windows of their apartment on the River Neva, Count Grabbe's sons watched as

"In the afternoon of March 11," Count Grabbe reports, "we went for a walk along the Bobrinsky Highway. Then there was tea and dinner as usual. Afterwards we played dominoes . . . as it turned out for the last time."

The Tsar, third from left, with members of his suite (1917)

170

streams of people stormed across the Liteiny Bridge — on their way to the Tauride Palace, seat of the Duma.

Meantime the Cabinet had adjourned the Duma for two months, but many delegates refused to leave. Senior members of the legislature organized themselves into a Provisional Committee — nucleus of the Provisional Government to come — for the purpose of restoring order at the capital. Most of the deputies were not radicals; they sought parliamentary government. But time was short. An unforeseen development was already posing a challenge to the authority of the new Provisional Committee of the Duma.

In a bold bid for power, a group of left-wing intellectuals, together with some workers' representatives, issued an appeal to the city's factories for the immediate election of delegates to Petrograd's Workers' Soviet. Within hours, 200 delegates assembled in a wing of the Tauride Palace. This Soviet, later expanded, would soon start wielding the real power in Russia.

That evening General Khabalov declared a state of siege. He still had 100,000 loyal troops, but with each passing hour their number dwindled. The Cabinet met in urgent session, and telegraphed the Tsar urging him to dispatch a general with troops to end the uprising. They waited in vain for an answer. After midnight the ministers dispersed, unaware that many of them would be arrested by the Provisional Committee the next day.

Thus ended the first day of the Revolution. The uprising had been swift, relatively bloodless, and confined almost exclusively to the capital. The rest of the country had not participated in the events of the day and knew as yet next to nothing of what had been going on.

In Mogilev on that critical Monday, March 12, 1917, Count Grabbe reports, "General Alekseiev came several times during the day to the governor's mansion with telegrams from Petrograd, where the situation is said to be very alarming.

"That evening, Count Fredericks and Voyeikov came while we were having tea and called the Tsar out into the adjoining room. We assumed that they wanted to tell him something especially important, for they usually never came at night. . . . When the Tsar came back into the dining room, it was barely noticeable that he was upset. . . . In about twenty minutes Count Fredericks and Voyeikov came again . . . and this time we took our leave.

"The *fligel adjutants* went to their quarters, but I waited in the room occupied by Dr. Feodorov, who had stayed upstairs in Voyeikov's quarters to find out what was up. In about thirty minutes, the doctor appeared on the run and called out to me when I asked what had happened: 'Tell you later. Now you'd better pack. We are leaving in an hour.'"

On the day the Revolution was gaining momentum at the capital,
the Tsar, Count Grabbe reports, surrounded by members of his
suite, waited for news at the governor's mansion in Mogilev.
Left to right: Colonel Mordvinov, Colonel Silaiev, Dr. Feodorov,
Prince Dolgoruky, Admiral Nilov, the Tsar, Count Grabbe (1917)

That night, after the members of his entourage had gone, the Tsar acted
with considerable determination. Concerned for the safety of his family,
so close to the mutinous capital, he ordered the Imperial train made ready
so he could leave for Tsarskoe without delay. He sent word to the Empress
to stay there until he came. He also ordered reliable troops headed by
General N. I. Ivanov, veteran soldier, to the capital to quell the disorders.

Despite General Alekseiev's plea that he remain in Mogilev and not take
the chance of being cut off from the army and the government, the Tsar
stuck to his decision to go.

"Actually," Count Grabbe relates, "we left Mogilev about six in the
morning of Tuesday, March 13, and it was only in the train that we
learned revolution had broken out in Petrograd. I must say, it is surprising

that one can be so close to the center of things, and yet find that everything is concealed. One learns of such momentous events almost by accident.

". . . The journey went routinely. As usual, officials of the provinces through which we were passing met the train. They came on board and gave the Tsar the latest news. At one point we stopped at a juncture where a troop train was waiting, and the soldiers on the troop train cheered loudly.

"At about four in the afternoon news came through that Duma deputy Bublikov had seized the Ministry of Transport. . . . Farther on, at Malaya Vishera, we learned that the towns of Lyuban and Tosno, directly ahead, were in the hands of mutineers. Railroad workers at this point disconnected the telegraph line to our train, cutting us off from the outside world. Whereupon the Tsar was awakened, and he ordered the train to turn back

General N. I. Ivanov, right. With him are members of the Allied military missions (1916).

Dispatched by the Tsar to the capital, Ivanov never got any farther than Tsarskoe Selo.

Like a hunted animal, the Imperial train was blocked en route to
Tsarskoe Selo and forced to backtrack (1917).

to Bologoye, which we had passed two hours earlier, and from there take
a side line to Pskov, headquarters of General N. V. Ruzsky, Commander
of the Northern Front.

"When the train reached Bologoye we raced past the station without
slowing down lest we be intercepted. From then on we proceeded with
great caution, stopping at every station to inquire if all was clear ahead.
. . . In this fashion we reached Pskov toward evening of March 14."

In Pskov the Tsar received General Ruzsky in the train. The general
briefed him on the critical situation at the capital and then tried to persuade
him to agree to some political concessions. He met with determined resis-
tance. Nicholas, according to Katkov, believed that "the transfer of power
to a government answering to parliament would in no way relieve him of
the responsibility for the actions of this government." Therefore his duty
before God was clear.

All that night General Ruzsky conferred by direct wire with M. V.
Rodzianko, the Duma head, in Petrograd. By morning it appeared that
only the Tsar's abdication would be sufficient to appease popular passions.
The text of this conversation was at once transmitted to General Alekseiev,

Count Grabbe and Grand Duke Michael Alexandrovich (1916)
    Grand Duke Michael Alexandrovich had stayed away from politics all his life. With the abdication of his brother he suddenly found himself heir to the throne. Uncertain what to do, he consulted Duma leaders and finally agreed to accept the crown, if chosen by a Constitutional Assembly soon to be called.

who thereupon communicated with the commanding generals at the various fronts. In his message he advised the generals, "A decision on the dynastic question is now demanded, and the war can be continued to a victorious end only if requests for the Emperor's abdication in his son's favor with Michael Alexandrovich acting as regent are satisfied." "Such," comments Count Grabbe, "was the directive [*ukazanie*] Alekseiev had received from Petrograd."

Answers from the commanders came in the early afternoon of the next day. The generals urged the Tsar to abdicate in favor of his son as they believed that such a step would save the monarchy and make it possible to continue the war. The Tsar took very seriously the advice of his generals. According to accounts of the scene, he strode to the window of the train and stood for a moment looking at the winter landscape. He then turned, made the sign of the cross, and announced his decision to abdicate in favor of his son. Later that day — March 15, 1917 — after conferring with Dr. Feodorov, who assured him that his son's illness was incurable, he abdicated also for Alexis and passed the crown to his brother, Grand Duke Michael Alexandrovich. As Pares reports, "Grand Duke Michael, next day, after taking advice, made his acceptance conditional on the request of a Constitutional Assembly, to be elected by universal franchise. That was actually the end of the Romanov dynasty," as the Bolshevik seizure of power intervened. Pares, who knew the Tsar personally, believes that in abdicating Nicholas felt he was acting in the best interests of the country.

To quote Paul Grabbe's memoirs, *Window on the River Neva*, page 123, "Though Father was in the same train, he was not present when Nicholas made this crucial decision. However, shortly afterwards he found himself alone with the Tsar in the dining car. They talked briefly over a glass of tea. In a matter-of-fact voice Nicholas said to Father: 'Now that I am about to be freed of my responsibilities to the nation, perhaps I can fulfill my life's desire — to have a farm, somewhere in England. What do you think?'

"To this seemingly casual question, Father reacted with long pent-up emotion. Only now — too late — was he being asked for his thoughts.

"'What do I think?' he exclaimed. 'What will become of you, of us, of

Railroad station at Mogilev (1916)
Dramatic action would occur here within days of the abdication.

176

Russia, now that those questionable characters are in control? Your Majesty, this is a tragic step you have taken. . . .'

"Father described the response to his outburst: Nicholas remained silent. His face showed no emotion, but as he left the dining car, Father observed, he seemed hurt."

Count Grabbe's notes continue: "That night our train got started and headed via Vitebsk to Mogilev. The mood of everybody in the train was one of deep dejection, and everyone speculated about the uncertain situation that had arisen, changing everything in the most fundamental way. For with the stroke of the pen, the Tsar had transformed himself from the ruler of all Russia to a person with no rights whatsoever, at the mercy of heaven only knows what questionable characters."

After his abdication, the former Emperor had been granted permission by the new regime to return to Mogilev to bid farewell to the troops before joining his family at Tsarskoe Selo. The evening following his return, the Dowager Empress Maria Feodorovna arrived by train from Kiev to say good-bye to her son. Grand Duke Alexander Mikhailovich accompanied her.

When Maria Feodorovna's train was brought to the Imperial platform, Nicholas entered his mother's car and spent two hours alone with her.

On the morning of Sunday, March 18, Nicholas went to mass at the cathedral, as was his custom. "He stood on the same spot as usual," says Count Grabbe, "and it was painful to watch him, especially when at one point in the service — the *Bolshoy Vykhod* — instead of using the customary words, 'devout and great Tsar of ours,' the deacon intoned something he had just newly concocted. Many people cried."

"The next day," Monday, March 19, Count Grabbe continues, "he sorted out his papers and after lunch went to a staff hall where all the military personnel serving at Headquarters had assembled."

Another eyewitness, the former Minister of Finance of the Imperial Government, later knighted Sir Peter Bark, describes the scene:

"The room was crowded; even the staircase and entrance hall were full of people. Conversation was in subdued tones and all eyes were turned towards the door through which the Emperor was to enter. Ten minutes passed, then rapid and light steps on the stairs were heard. There was a complete silence followed by the command: 'On guard!' The Emperor, wearing a Cossack uniform, entered quietly and advanced to the center of the hall.

"The Emperor remained silent for some moments, then, amid perfect stillness, he spoke in his clear, sonorous voice. He said that he submitted to God's will and was laying down his post as Supreme Commander.

The cathedral at Mogilev (1916)

. . . He cordially thanked the whole staff for its work and expressed the conviction that Russia and her Allies would be victorious and that Russia's sacrifices had not been in vain. . . . Since the first words were pronounced by the Emperor, tears had risen to the eyes of the listeners . . . and all those present felt the same emotion experienced when death brings final parting from a loved one."

In his journal Count Grabbe tells of a dramatic incident that occurred the following day when men from the *Konvoy* regiment were called out to defend their former Tsar.

"Toward evening," he recalls, "I was informed that a large contingent of mutinous troops was preparing to detrain at Mogilev and then, early next morning, march towards the Governor's mansion. In this emergency I ordered two *Konvoy* squadrons to be alerted. They stationed themselves along the road leading from the station in order to block the approach of the mutinous troops, whose intentions evidently were unfriendly.

"The frame of mind of the officers and men was such that under no circumstances would they have let the revolutionary troops reach the Tsar and certainly would rather have perished. On learning of this deployment of *Konvoy* Cossacks in the path of their march, the mutinous troops hesitated, then hastily withdrew." Ironically, the men of the *Konvoy* would be

178

Four of the 200 *Konvoy* horsemen who blocked the approach of mutinous troops to the governor's mansion in Mogilev (1917)

powerless to protect Nicholas from the real threat to his life in the months ahead.

Then came the last day in Mogilev, Wednesday, March 21. "In the morning after tea," Count Grabbe recalls, "the Tsar prepared for his journey. He said good-bye to the *Konvoy* personnel, thanking them for their service, then went to [the train occupied by his mother] Maria Feodorovna where he awaited the time of departure.

"On this day the Tsar wrote his last message to the troops, Order #321."

> Today I am addressing for the last time my dearly loved armies. I have abdicated for myself and for my son, and I am leaving the throne of the Emperors of Russia. The supreme power has passed over to the Provisional Government formed by the Duma of the Empire. May the Savior help this government to lead Russia towards glory and success! May God help you also, my brave soldiers, to preserve our country from a cruel enemy! . . .

This last order of the day from the former sovereign to his soldiers never reached them. "In accordance with instructions from the new War Minister, Gutchkov," says Count Grabbe, "it was never published nor distributed to the troops by General Alekseiev."

179

In his journal, Count Grabbe departs from his usual commentary to pass judgment on the actions of General Alekseiev: "General Alekseiev, in view of the situation, hastened to return from the Crimea [where he was convalescing] to Headquarters and relieved General Gurko [his deputy]. What a pity that Gurko was unable to await [in his post] the arrival of the Tsar to Headquarters; most importantly, that he had to yield his post to Alekseiev [of leftist tendencies]. For under him, everything would probably have come out quite differently."

Here is the original passage in Russian:

Later on, Count Grabbe added: "In justice to General Alekseiev, one must acknowledge that he quickly perceived all the falsity of his politics; that within 48 hours he had a change of mind, but it was already too late. The forward sweep of events had by then become irresistible."

At 3 P.M. a special train arrived from Petrograd, bearing the representatives of the Provisional Government, A. A. Bublikov and N. V. Nekrasov, both Duma deputies who had been delegated to bring the Tsar back to the capital. "They took over all the arrangements for the journey," says Count Grabbe, "and indicated who would be allowed to accompany the Tsar." Reliable revolutionary guards were stationed inside each carriage.

Among those excluded was Count Grabbe, no doubt because he was the only member of the entourage who commanded a military force capable of stopping the train.

Why didn't he do so? As he notes in his journal, neither he nor anyone else at Mogilev except General Alekseiev knew that the former emperor was under arrest. What he did know was that Nicholas had asked everyone to obey the Provisional Government and that he was intent on rejoining his family at Tsarskoe Selo.

Why didn't Count Grabbe try to escort the former emperor? He later

Nicholas II at the window of the Imperial train (1916)

told his family that such an act would have been a futile gesture, a mere play to the gallery. He knew that if he tried to board the train he would have been removed by the revolutionary guards.

Later, recalling the departure of Nicholas from general headquarters, Count Grabbe says: "The train of Maria Feodorovna stood on an adjoining track, and it is hard to think back to that terrible moment when the Tsar, after saying good-bye to his mother forever, stepped across to his own train, where he found himself at the complete mercy of the deputies who had come to take him away.

"As soon as the Tsar entered his train it rolled out of the Mogilev station. The time was 3:45 P.M."

# *Epilogue*

Barely a week after his abdication, the former Emperor was taken to Tsarskoe Selo, where he rejoined his family in the Alexander Palace. They were kept there under house arrest until August 1, when the Provisional Government, fearing for their safety, transferred the prisoners to Tobolsk, Siberia, remote from revolutionary turmoil. A few attendants were allowed to accompany them.

After the Leninist coup, the Soviet government moved the captives in April 1918 to the Ipatiev house in Ekaterinburg, seat of the Ural Soviet.

Three months later, when anti-Bolshevik forces approached from the east, the decision was made in Moscow by Lenin and his associate, Sverdlov, to do away with a potential focus for rallying anti-Revolutionary forces.

On the night of July 16, 1918, the family was assembled in the basement of the Ipatiev house and shot, ostensibly by order of the Ural Soviet. The name of the town was later changed to Sverdlovsk.

News of the multiple assassination, when it came, was deliberately falsified by the Soviet government, presumably to avoid admitting that the Empress and the children had also been killed.

## MASSACRE IN EKATERINBURG

*The New York Times* in good faith reprinted the only news coming out of Russia regarding the Tsar's execution, quoting a Moscow communiqué by wireless to London on July 20, 1918. The announcement was deliberately misleading.

No doubt fearing world reaction, the Moscow authorities at first concealed the whole grisly truth: that the former emperor and his entire family and attendants had been gunned down on the night of July 16/17 in an Ekaterinburg cellar.

Another attempt by Moscow to mislead is the impression created by the official announcement that the Ural Soviet gave the order. Actually, as Leon Trotsky reports in his book entitled *Diary in Exile, 1935,* published in 1953, it was Lenin and Jacob Sverdlov, a key Bolshevik organizer, who

# EX-CZAR OF RUSSIA KILLED BY ORDER OF URAL SOVIET

## Nicholas Shot on July 16 When It Was Feared That Czecho-slovaks Might Seize Him.

### WIFE AND HEIR IN SECURITY

#### Bolshevist Government Approves Act. Alleging Plot for a Counter-Revolution.

### PRISONER'S PAPERS SEIZED

#### Former Emperor's Diary and Letters from Rasputin Soon to be Made Public.

LONDON, July 20.—Nicholas Romanoff, ex-Czar of Russia, was shot July 16, according to a Russian announcement by wireless today.

The former Empress and Alexis Romanoff, the young heir, have been sent to a place of security.

The message announces that a counter-revolutionary conspiracy was discovered, with the object of wresting the ex-Emperor from the authority of the Soviet Council. In view of this fact and

made the decision in Moscow. Trotsky quotes Sverdlov as telling him, "We decided here. Ilyich [Lenin] believed that we shouldn't leave the Whites a live banner to rally around. . . ."

Lenin and Sverdlov also apparently made the decision to change the wording of the original announcement by the Ural Soviet. As can be seen in the official document reproduced on the next page, all reference to Nicholas's family and their burial has been crossed out. The handwritten statement declares that publication of the deleted sections is forbidden.

# ЭКСТРЕННЫЙ ВЫПУСК

По распоряжению Областого
Исполнительного Комитета Советов
Рабочих, Крестьянских и Солдатских
Депутатов Урала и Рев. Штаба бывший

**Царь и Самодержавец**
**Николай Романов**

расстрелян ~~~~~~~~~~~~
17 июля 1918 года.

~~~~~~~~~~~~

Председатель ....дома
Белобородов

г. Екатеринбург, 20 - июля 1918 г.
10 часов утра

Экстренный выпускъ отъ 20 июля 1918 года
съ сообщениемъ о разстрѣлѣ Царской Семьи

The typewritten document was issued by the Ural Soviet to announce the execution of Nicholas II. The translation is given below.

## SPECIAL BULLETIN

By order of the Executive Committee of the Ural Workers'

Peasants' and Soldiers' Deputies, and the Revolutionary Staff,

the former

Tsar and Autocrat

Nicholas Romanov

has been shot together with his family [*Last four words are*

*crossed out*] on July 17, 1918.

The bodies have been given burial [*Entire sentence crossed*

*out*] "Publication prohibited." [*Written in ink across document*

*over illegible signature*]

Chairman of the Revolutionary Committee

Beloborodov

[Official stamp of the

Revolutionary Committee]

The Town of Ekaterinburg, July 20, 1918,
10 a.m.

# *Notes*

## PART I   RUSSIA IN THE EARLY TWENTIETH CENTURY

1   Highest rate of industrial growth: McKay, pp. 4–5.
    More than half were serfs: Pipes, chart, p. 145.
2   "necessity to decentralize": Von Mohrenschildt, *Toward a United States of Russia*,
    p. 254.
    By 1917 about 45 percent literate: Timasheff, p. 83.
    Zemstvo assemblies "created . . . real self-government": Vernadsky, p. 24.
    Until 1906 the peasant could not leave the village without permission: Pipes,
    p. 169.
    "the most prosperous period in Russian history": Pares, *The Fall of the Russian
    Monarchy*, p. 115.
C10 Christianity brought to Russia in A.D. 988: Mirsky, p. 37.
19  "According to custom [the ball] was opened": Meriel Buchanan, p. 87.
23  Trotsky and the first "soviet": Lincoln, *The Romanovs*, p. 657.
24  "Because nine-tenths of the troublemakers": N to MF, pp. 190–191 (October 27,
    1905, O.S.).
    "One could see political confidence": Pares, *The Fall of the Russian Monarchy*, p. 118.
26  "amelioration": Morton, p. 192.
    United States Congress abrogates treaty: *Congressional Record*, vol. 48. pt. 1 (Dec.
    20, 1911), p. 559.
    "with more valor than discretion": Tuchman, p. 57.
    Agree to mobilize in fifteen days: ibid., p. 57.
    Inadequacies of Minister for War General Sukhomlinov, ibid., p. 61; Mazour,
    pp. 400–401.

## PART II   THE TSAR AND HIS FAMILY

29  "took his role as God's representative": Mosolov, p. 10.
30  "conviction that all his decisions": Katkov, p. 353.
    "His serenity was based on the conviction": ibid., p. 354.
    "proved disastrous in the conditions": ibid., p. 355.
    "remarkable clearness of head": Kokovtsev, quoted by Pares, *The Fall of the Russian
    Monarchy*, p. 129.
    "a great sense of order": ibid., p. 129.
    The Tsar's "conquering personal charm": ibid., p. 31.
33  "a fine, gallant old gentleman": Hanbury-Williams, p. 165.
C37 "exercise was an absolute necessity": Pares, *The Fall of the Russian Monarchy*, p. 32.

C39    "to whom he was at once Emperor, father and comrade": ibid., p. 129.

41    "How I thought of darling Alicky": Journal of Queen Victoria quoted by Buckle, II, 454.

42    "I knew her good qualities . . .": Buxhoeveden, pp. v–vi.

"acted largely on impulse": ibid., p. 233.

"when he disagreed": ibid., p. 232.

43    "a handsome woman in the florid style . . .": ibid., p. 172.

"unpretentious and guileless": ibid., p. 171.

"unwittingly harmed the Empress": ibid., p. 172.

"From her [the Empress's] intense love . . .": ibid., p. v.

Only Vyrubova and the Empress believed in Rasputin: ibid., p. 144.

C44    "the Tsar's favorite picture": ibid., p. 97.

C46    "The Tsar is a saint and an angel": Grand Duke Ernest Louis of Hesse-Darmstadt to Sazanov, quoted by Pares, p. 49.

50    "so many precious gifts": Gilliard, p. 40.

"had very quick wits": ibid., p. 40.

C54    "He thoroughly enjoyed life": ibid., p. 40.

C64    "allowed to have a little preference": Vyrubova, pp. 79–80.

69    "What a bundle of mischief": Grand Duchess Olga Alexandrovna, quoted by Vorres, p. 102.

Bykov confirmed Sokolov re assassination of entire family: Sokolov and Bykov reports; Massie, p. 495.

## PART III   VACATIONING WITH THE TSAR, 1912–1914

75    Family hoped to be allowed to live in Livadia: Buxhoeveden, p. 304.

76    "white mosques standing out against the old cypresses": Gilliard, p. 91.

77    Golitzin willing estate and vineyard to Tsar: Buxhoeveden, p. 178.

91    "I never heard the slightest word": Mosolov, p. 247.

C111    "My daughter-in-law does not like me . . .": Kokovtsev, p. 470.

## PART IV   THE LAST YEARS OF THE REGIME

121    "It is difficult to believe": N to AF, October 5, 1914.

C126    "Have spent an ever-memorable day": N to AF, December 14, 1914.

C133    "did everyone good": Buxhoeveden, p. 218.

"used to lie like lizards": ibid., p. 218.

C134    "Where are you?": Count Grabbe's notes.

137    "threatens with serious consequences": Pares, *The Fall of the Russian Monarchy*, p. 270.

140    "During the night the boy got worse": Gilliard, pp. 155–156.

142    Fifteen million men mobilized: Charques, p. 231; Mazour, p. 411.

143    Attempts "to induce the Emperor to steer a more liberal course": Sir George Buchanan, II, 4.

"in the periods of what may be called his good health": Hanbury-Williams, p. 237.

"As time went on": ibid., pp. 238–239.

144　"came out of his father's room": ibid., p. 138.
144　"With a candor that utterly amazed me": Gilliard, pp. 167–168.
　　"He spoke roughly to Alexis": ibid., p. 178.
159　"It was a gray, windy day of April": Meriel Buchanan, pp. 138–139.
　　"at one and the same time ignorant and eloquent": Beletsky, verbatim, in *La Chute du régime tsariste*, p. 1.
　　"possessing unusual peasant shrewdness": Charques, p. 196.
161　"always managed to come when there was a tendency": Buxhoeveden, p. 141.
163　"You may be quite sure": N to AF, September 8, 1916.
　　Two irate husbands: Fülöp-Miller, p. 294.
166　"proving yourself the autocrat": AF to N, September 5, 1915.
　　"Yes, truly, you ought to be my eyes": N to AF, October 6, 1916.
　　Seventeen ministers dismissed in 1916: Katkov, chart, p. 434.
　　Rasputin able to halt the offensive: Pares, *The Fall of the Russian Monarchy*, p. 368.
　　"mean spirit, low character": Paléologue, III, 30.
　　"'She has come again it appears'": Vyrubova, p. 140.
168　Shocked by the Tsar's haggard appearance: Kokovtsev, p. 478.
　　"now resigned to disaster": Paléologue, III, 152.
169　"an excruciating pain in the chest": N to AF, March 11, 1917.
　　Symptoms of a heart attack: Massie, p. 390.
174　"transfer of power . . . would in no way relieve": Katkov, p. 322.
175　"A decision on the dynastic question . . .": ibid., pp. 331 ff.
176　"Grand Duke Michael, next day": Pares, *Russia*, p. 86.
177　"The room was crowded": Bark, pp. 75ff.
179　Order #321 of the former Tsar: ibid., p. 84.

EPILOGUE

183　Quotes Sverdlov telling him, "We decided here": Trotsky, p. 81.

# Bibliography

Alexandra, Tsarina of Russia, *Letters of the Tsaritsa to the Tsar 1914–1916* (London: Duckworth, 1923). (Cited in Notes as AF to N.)

Bark, Sir Peter, "The Last Days of the Russian Monarchy: Nicholas II at Army Headquarters," *The Russian Revolution, 1917: Contemporary Accounts*, ed. Dimitri Von Mohrenschildt (London, New York: Oxford University Press, 1971).

Benckendorff, Count Paul, *Last Days at Tsarskoe Selo* (London: Heinemann, 1927).

Bing, Edward J., ed., *The Secret Letters of the Last Tsar: The Confidential Correspondence between Nicholas II and His Mother, Dowager Empress Marie Feodorovna* (New York: Longmans, Green, 1938). (Cited in Notes as N to MF.)

*Bolshaia sovetskaia entziklopedia* (Large Soviet Encyclopedia) (Moscow: State Publishing House, 1953), vol. 38.

Buchanan, Sir George, *My Mission to Russia*, 2 vols. (London, New York: Cassell, 1923).

Buchanan, Meriel (Mrs. Knowling), *The Dissolution of an Empire* (London: Murray, 1932; reprinted in Russia Observed series, New York: Arno Press, 1971).

Buxhoeveden, Baroness Sophie, *The Life and Tragedy of Alexandra Feodorovna, Empress of Russia: A Biography* (New York, London: Longmans, Green, 1928).

Bykov, P. M., *The Last Days of Tsardom* (London: Martin Lawrence, 1937).

Charques, Richard, *The Twilight of Imperial Russia* (London: Oxford University Press, 1965).

La Chute. See *Padenie*

*Congressional Record*, vol. 48, pt. 1 (Washington, D.C.: U.S. Government Printing Office, 1911).

Cowles, Virginia, *The Last Tsar* (New York: Putnam, 1977). First American edition.

Crankshaw, Edward, *The Shadow of the Winter Palace: Russia's Drift to Revolution 1825–1917* (New York: Viking, 1976).

*The Encyclopaedia Britannica*, 11th ed. (Cambridge: Cambridge University Press, 1911), vols. 6, 19, 23.

*Entsiklopedicheskii slovar Brokgaus & Efron* (Brokgaus & Efron Russian Encyclopedia) (St. Petersburg, 1903), vol. 74.

*Entsiklopedicheskii slovar russkogo bibliograficheskogo Instituta Granat* (Granat Russian Encyclopedia) (Moscow: Academia Nauk, SSSR, 1929).

Florinsky, Michael T., *The End of the Russian Empire* (New Haven: Yale University Press, 1931).

———, *Russia: A History and an Interpretation*, 2 vols. (New York: Macmillan, 1955).

Fülöp-Miller, René, *Rasputin: The Holy Devil* (New York: Garden City, 1928).

Galushkin, Colonel N. V., compiler, *Sobstveny ego imperatorgskago velichestva Konvoy* (His Imperial Majesty's Konvoy) (San Francisco: B. V. Charsky, 1961).

Gilliard, Pierre, *Thirteen Years at the Russian Court* (New York: Doran, 1921; reprint, Russia Observed series, New York: Arno Press, 1970).

Golovine, General N. N., *The Russian Army in the World War* (New Haven: Yale University

Press, 1931; London: Oxford University Press, 1931; reprint, New York: Anchor Books, 1969).

Grabbe, General Count Alexander, "Notes" (in manuscript).

Hanbury-Williams, Major General Sir John, *The Emperor Nicholas II as I Knew Him* (New York: Dutton, 1928).

*Jane's Fighting Ships* (London: Sampson Low, 1914–1935).

Katkov, George, *Russia 1917: The February Revolution* (New York: Harper & Row, 1967).

Knox, Major General Sir Alfred, *With the Russian Army, 1914–1917* (New York: Dutton, 1921; reprinted in Russia Observed series, New York: Arno Press, 1971).

Kokovtsev, Count Vladimir, *Out of My Past: The Memoirs of Count Kokovtsev* (Stanford: Stanford University Press, 1935).

Lincoln, W. Bruce, *In War's Dark Shadow: The Russians before the Great War* (New York: Dial, 1983).

————, *The Romanovs* (New York: Dial Press, 1981).

Maklakov, V. A., *Iz vospominany* (From My Memoirs) (New York: Chekhov Publishing House of the East European Fund, Inc., 1954).

Massie, Robert K., *Nicholas and Alexandra* (New York: Atheneum, 1967).

Mazour, Anatole G., *Russia Past and Present* (New York: Van Nostrand, 1951).

McKay, John P., *Pioneers for Profit: Foreign Entrepreneurship and Russian Industrialization 1885–1913* (Chicago: University of Chicago Press, 1970).

Melgunov, S. P., *Na putyakh k dvorzovomu perevorotu* (On the Road to the Palace Revolution) (Paris: Librairie La Source, 1931).

Miliukov, P. N., *Vospominania, 1859–1917* (Memoirs, 1859–1917), 2 vols. (New York: Chekhov, 1955).

Mirsky, Prince D. S., *Russia: A Social History* (New York: Century, 1930).

Mohrenschildt, Dimitri Von, ed., *The Russian Revolution of 1917: Contemporary Accounts* (New York, London: Oxford University Press, 1971).

————, *Toward a United States of Russia: Plans and Projects of Federal Reconstruction of Russia in the Nineteenth Century* (London, Toronto: Fairleigh Dickinson University Press/ Associated University Presses, 1981).

(Mosolov) Mossolov, A. A., *At the Court of the Last Tsar* (London: Methuen, 1935).

Morton, Frederic, *The Rothschilds: A Family Portrait* (New York: Atheneum, 1962).

Nicholas, Tsar of Russia, *Letters of the Tsar to the Tsaritsa 1914–1917* (London: Bodley Head; New York: Dodd, Mead, 1929). (Cited in Notes as N to AF.)

*Padenie tsarskogo regima*, 7 vols. (Moscow: Gosizdat, 1924–1927). Extracts trans. in French: *La Chute du régime tsariste, interrogatoires* (Paris: Payot, 1927).

Paléologue, Maurice, *La Russie des tsars pendant la grande guerre*, 3 vols. (Paris: Librairie Plon, 1921; trans. as *An Ambassador's Memoirs*, 3 vols.; New York, Doran, 1925).

Pares, Sir Bernard, *The Fall of the Russian Monarchy* (New York: Vintage Books, 1961).

————, *Russia* (New York: Penguin Books, 1943).

Pipes, Richard, *Russia under the Old Regime* (New York: Scribner's, 1974).

Salisbury, Harrison E., *Russia in Revolution, 1900–1930* (New York: Holt, Rinehart & Winston, 1978).

Sazonov, Serge, *Fateful Years* (New York: Stokes, 1928).

Seton-Watson, Hugh, *The Russian Empire 1801–1917* (London: Oxford University Press, 1967).

Sokolov, Nicolas, *Enquête judiciare sur l'assassinat de la famille impériale russe* (Paris: Payot, 1924).

Timasheff, N. S., "Overcoming Illiteracy: Public Education in Russia, 1880–1914," *The Russian Review*, (Autumn 1942).

Tokmakoff, George, *P. A. Stolypin and the Third Duma* (Washington, D.C.: University Press of America, 1981).

Tolstoy, Count Leo, *War and Peace*, trans. Constance Garnett (New York: Random House Modern Library, 1961).

Trotsky, Leon, *Trotsky's Diary in Exile: 1935*, trans. Elena Zarudnaya (Cambridge, Mass.: Harvard University Press, 1958).

Troyat, Henri, *Daily Life in Russia under the Last Tsar* (New York: Macmillan, 1962).

Tuchman, Barbara W., *The Guns of August* (New York: Macmillan, 1962).

Vernadsky, George, *A History of Russia* (New Haven: Yale University Press, 1954).

Victoria, Queen of England, *Letters of Queen Victoria*, ed. George Earle Buckle, 3 vols. (3d series, London: Murray, 1931).

Vorres, Ian, *The Last Grand Duchess: The Memoirs of Grand Duchess Olga Alexandrovna* (New York: Scribner's, 1964).

(Vyrubova) Viroubova, Anna, *Memories of the Russian Court* (New York: Macmillan, 1923).

Wallace, Sir Donald Mackenzie, *Russia on the Eve of War and Revolution*, ed. Cyril E. Black (New York: Vintage Books, 1961).

Warner, Marina, *Queen Victoria's Sketchbook* (New York: Crown, 1979).